Self Help Mindfulness

Learn How to Change Your Mind and Stop Being Anxio[illegible] Nothing and Beat Anxiety and Depressio[illegible]itation for Better Focus and

Chapter 1: What Is Mindfulness

The human mind gets distracted easily. It habitually examines past events and tries to anticipate future ones. You may think that being aware of your feelings, sensations, and thoughts is not a good idea. However, doing that in a way that suspend self-criticism and judgment may have a good impact on your life.

Mindfulness is basically the practice of becoming completely aware of the present instead of dwelling on the past or venturing into the future. It is a way of clearly seeing and paying attention to what is happening around you. While it cannot get rid of the pressure you experience, it can help you respond to it in a better and calmer manner.

Mindfulness can help you recognize and stay away from unconscious physiological and emotional reactions to daily events. It can provide you with a scientific approach to cultivating insight, understanding, and clarity. When you practice mindfulness, you will be able to be completely present in your life, and even improve its quality.

Mindfulness involves an increased awareness of sensory stimuli, so you really notice the sensations in your body and your breathing. You can achieve mindfulness through meditation, although you can also practice it through your daily living by focusing on the current situation and quieting your inner thoughts.

Mindfulness is actually a simple form of meditation. It is about observation with the absence of criticism and being compassionate with yourself. It lets you focus on your breathing as it flows throughout your body. When you focus on every breath, you are able to observe the thoughts in your head.

You are able to realize that these thoughts come and go, and that you are not really your thoughts. You are able to come to an understanding that feelings and thoughts are transient. You actually have the ability to choose whether or not you will act on these feelings and thoughts.

What Mindfulness Entails, Who Is It For, and How Is It Practiced?

Jon Kabat-Zinn states that mindfulness is about paying attention in a certain way without judgment, with a purpose, and in the present moment. Those who practice it learn how to pay attention on purpose by practicing especially created mindfulness meditation practices and mindful movements.

The practitioners can learn how to stop or slow down thoughts and reactions with adequate practice. This will allow them to experience the present moment as it is. Everyone has a tendency to harbor uninvited thoughts into their heads no matter how much they practice mindfulness.

This is alright, though. It is not really what your brain does that matters, but rather how you respond to its thoughts. If you begin to think about your thoughts or get frustrated with yourself for not being able to stay focused, you will lose your attention from the present moment.

On the other hand, if you acknowledge your thoughts and let them go without judgment, you will be able to retain your focus on staying in the present moment. Just like new skills, the more you practice this, the easier it will be for you to do it over and over. Basically, the more you practice mindfulness, the more you develop neuro-pathways in your brain and the easier it will be for you to stay in the present moment.

When you learn to experience the present moment, you are able to move away from unconscious and habitual physiological and emotional reactions to daily events as well as view things as they really are. You are also able to respond to these things wisely instead of being on auto pilot.

Mindfulness is for people of all ages, gender, or status. It is not a religion, so it does not really matter what your religious component is. Anyone can have the benefits of mindfulness, regardless of their belief system. Mindfulness actually has powerful medicinal benefits.

The most researched and recognized modern forms of mindfulness are MBCT and MBSR. These programs are typically taught for eight weeks, and the participants are asked to meet for two to three hours per week. There are also home practices in between the meetings.

The participants are taught numerous meditation practices that have already been proven to help lessen brain chatter as well as respond more easily to feelings and thoughts. Most MBCT and MBSR trainings include body scan exercises, walking meditation, sitting meditation, body awareness exercises, gentle stretching, and mindfulness meditation.

The Benefits of Mindfulness

According to research, mindfulness has plenty of benefits. For instance, mindfulness-based stress reduction (MBSR) and mindfulness-based cognitive therapy (MBCT) have found to be helpful with anxiety disorders, including generalized anxiety disorder, depression, relationships, sleeping, eating disorders, and stress management.

Anxiety disorders, such as generalized anxiety disorder or GAD may be reduced with mindfulness-based intervention. With the use of such method, patients with anxiety disorders can efficiently lessen their depressive and anxiety symptoms.

Likewise, patients suffering from depression can benefit from mindfulness-based interventions. Those with residual depressive symptoms and depressive episodes can reduce their ruminations and symptoms. Better results can be seen after a month.

According to a certain study, people with greater mindfulness tend to have better and more satisfying relationships as well as able to deal more constructively with stress. According to another study, people who practice mindfulness have less stress when faced with conflicting situations. They are also able to communicate better.

Both of these studies have linked mindfulness with better relationships.

With regard to sleeping and eating disorders, mindfulness have also been found to be beneficial. Cancer patients, for instance, were able to reduce their sleep disturbance while improving the quality of their sleep.

Similarly, people with eating disorders are able to improve their condition. A group of women with bulimia nervosa underwent a mindfulness-based treatment program for eight weeks, and they were able to report significant improvements in their behaviors and emotions. They were also able to have greater compassion, self-awareness, and acceptance.

Furthermore, mindfulness can help people deal with stress better. Studies have found that mindfulness can help with daily stresses and more serious stresses, including life-threatening illnesses that are related to stress.

According to studies, mindfulness is beneficial in stopping ruminations over the things that result in stress. It basically helps people avoid harboring negative thoughts, as well as being anxious towards the future. It provides a break from stressful thought activities and even allows you to gain perspective.

Over time, mindfulness can cause long-term mood changes. Scientific studies show that mindfulness can prevent depression, and positively affect brain patterns associated with stress, anxiety, irritability, and depression. Other studies have also shown that people who regularly meditate require medical attention less frequently.

In addition, they become more creative, their memory improves, and their responses become faster. They are able to achieve resilience at home and work, as well as balance. Also, they are able to view situations more clearly. They recognize, stop, or slow down habitual and automatic reactions.

Myths with Regard to Mindfulness

Unfortunately, some people still have wrong notions regarding mindfulness. These people need to be educated properly regarding mindfulness-based interventions, so they can live more efficiently and happily.

Some people think that meditation is a religion. Well, this is not true because mindfulness is just mental training. Although a lot of those who practice meditation are religious, mindfulness is still not a religion. In fact, there are a lot of agnostics and atheists who also practice mindfulness.

Another false notion with regard to mindfulness is that meditators need to sit cross-legged on the floor. Well, meditators usually sit cross-legged, but this is not a requirement. You can actually sit on a chair if you do not feel comfortable sitting on the ground. You can even practice mindfulness while on a bus, train, or basically anywhere.

You do not have to spend an entire day practicing mindfulness. A lot of people refuse to practice mindfulness because they think that they are too busy. What they do not realize is that mindfulness does not require a lot of time. It can actually liberate you from the pressures of time, so you will have more of it.

There is nothing complicated about meditation. It is not even about failure or success. Even if it seems difficult, it will teach you valuable things regarding how your mind works. Hence, it will benefit you psychologically. Meditation will not prevent you from achieving important lifestyle or career goals.

Do not worry because it will not trick you into adopting a Pollyanna behavior towards life. It is not about accepting what is unacceptable. Meditation is about viewing the world with great clarity so you can make wise decisions. It will help you make the appropriate action with regard to things that you have to change.

Meditation can help you become more compassionate and more aware of your goals and values. It has also been clinically proven to be effective in fighting against stress, anxiety, depression, and exhaustion. It even works for people who are not depressed but are struggling to keep up with the high demands of society.

Chapter 2: Exercises

When our mind feels as if it's constantly being pulled from every corner, our thoughts become scattered and chaotic which in turn, affects the way we feel. This could leave us feeling overwhelmed and completely exhausted. In some cases, it can also make us feel irritable and easily angered, causing our tempers to flare up unnecessarily which, if left unchecked, can even damage our relationships.

Typically, the solution for this is to take some time off and get away from everything. However, not everyone can afford this luxury. For a lot of us, working continuously is a basic demand and taking care of our well-being becomes the least of our priorities. Now, you don't need a lengthy vacation to keep your mental health in check. All you really need is about 10 to 30 minutes of free time to indulge in a healing meditation that will put you back in a relaxed and mindful state.

It doesn't take a lot and this particular amount of time will not eat too much into your daily schedule. Remember, it is essential to put ourselves first, lest we end up burning out and being unable to do anything at all. Take care of your mind and body by doing these simple exercises everyday.

Mindful Breathing

When it comes to doing this exercise, note that you have the option to do it whilst standing up or sitting down. You can do it just about anywhere at any given time, as long as you're able to focus your mind and be still. Your concentration should all be on your breath for at least one whole minute.

Start breathing in and out slowly. A cycle of this should last for about 6 seconds. Breathe in through your nose and exhale through your mouth, allowing the air to flow freely into your body. Let go of any thoughts that you have, any pending projects or task that you still need to do. Be still.

This is the simplest form of meditation.

Mindful Observation

Simple yet very powerful, this exercise truly allows you to be in the moment and is designed to help you reconnect with the environment that you are in. Best done in the outdoors, this will enable you to better appreciate the beauty of the small things you often miss due to your everyday rush. It could be anything from the beautiful view of the city that you pass during commutes or something simpler, such as a garden that you see everyday but rarely pause for. It can also be applied during more relaxed moments; whilst you're on vacation and wanting to savor every moment of it.

To begin, simply pick a natural object within your surroundings. Focus on it and simply watch it for a minute or two. Allow yourself to fall into a relaxing state of mind, explore the image and take in even the smallest detail. As you do this, imagine your energy merging with this object. Connect with it and its simplicity of simply being.

Mindful Awareness

This particular exercise is meant to help us develop better appreciation and awareness when it comes to our daily tasks as well as its results.

To begin, think of something that's an everyday occurrence. A small thing that you often take for granted such as opening the windows at morning, watering the plants and even the mere act of sweeping. The next time you do any of these things, pay attention to what you're doing - to the way the air feels on your face when you open the window, the smell of the plants after you water them and the sound of the broom while you sweep. Focus on these things and allow it to take you away while you do the task. It's simple, but you'll definitely feel better about doing these things after.

Mindful Listening

Aside from using your sense of sight to develop mindfulness, you can also make use of your sense of hearing to further immerse yourself in this state of mind. This exercise is designed to enable you to open your ears to different sounds and listen in a non-judgmental way. Did you know that a lot of what we hear on a daily basis are influenced by past experiences?

To prevent fear, worry and anxiety due to this, we must learn how to listen while being neutral about it. To be aware, but to hear things without any preconceived notions.

To begin, choose music that you have never listened to before. Put on your headphones and listen to it. Don't think about anything else about it other than the sound you're hearing. If you happen to dislike it, let go of this feeling and allow the music to take over your thoughts.

Mindful Immersion

For this, the goal is to cultivate our contentment of the quiet moments and not chase after the adrenaline we get from always being busy. It's about being still and not looking for anything to do, simply enjoying the silence and allowing our mind to relax from the everyday chaos that it goes through. In doing this, we can avoid the anxiousness associated with wanting to finish tasks or catching up with deadlines. It provides clarity and restores our focus so that we can do more in the present.

Example, while you're making food for yourself or your family, try and focus on every detail of the task. Instead of rushing through it mindlessly, think about your ingredients and the process of preparation. By doing this, not only are you being present; you will also find better and more efficient ways of doing things. It's as if you're rediscovering the activity and experiencing it for the first time again.

This takes out the tediousness of doing something fairly routine and makes everything a lot more enjoyable.

Mindful Appreciation

For this, what you need to do is take note of 5 different things that happen in your daily life. These need to be things that typically go unappreciated or something that you don't really give much thought to. The goal here is to instil a sense of appreciation and gratitude for the small things in your life. These are the people or things that provide you with comfort and support whenever you need it, but also get neglected as you search for bigger things.

For example: take note of the person who delivers your mail or your daily paper, think of the clothes that give you warmth or the birds that sing to you each morning. Now ask yourself these questions:

Are you aware of how these things came to be and how they work?

Have you ever acknowledged how these small things benefit your life as well as that of others?

Can you imagine life without these things?

Have you paid attention to how complex these things are and that they have finer details that you once missed?

Have you ever spent time thinking about how these things connect with you and the environment? Ever thought of the role they play when it comes to the bigger picture?

Why do this? It may not seem like much at first, but repetition will help you develop a better appreciation and understanding of the environment around you. This also includes better self-awareness as you're able to tune out what's not needed and focus more on the things that matter. It's all about really seeing the world around you without any judgment or bias, to simply appreciate things as they were created.

The Importance of Unlocking Your Untapped Power

Before we discuss ways to eliminate stress, improve your confidence, and work on the key traits you need to fulfill your goals and be successful, we must discuss why unlocking your untapped power is important.

In this chapter, we shall discuss why you need to tap into your hidden potential and unlock it; we shall follow this with a discussion on how stress hinders your goal accomplishment.

Why You Need To Reach Your Full Potential

Each of us has certain goals and aspirations we desire to achieve. Some want to become wealthy while others dream of having a loving family. Although we set many goals, we often fail to accomplish them as planned. This mainly happens because we lack the key ingredients needed to fulfill our goals.

To achieve your goals and become successful, you need an optimistic mindset, unwavering self-confidence, strong will, determination to move forward, perseverance, ability to set meaningful goals, and the habit to stick to your mission until you fulfill it.

To achieve success in everything you do, you need to develop these qualities and character traits. To do that, you MUST unlock your full potential and untapped power. The power you need to be amazing is already within you: it is something you are born with. However, and this is the most unfortunate part, the societal norms and traditions you follow often enslave you to traditions that cause you to forget and forsake your true power.

To make your life meaningful, do everything you desire, and be the boss of your life, you MUST unlock your full potential so you can be the best you. Unlocking your full potential and tapping into your untapped power helps you become optimistic, truly confident, creative, resilient, courageous, and gritty; these are the key elements you need to become successful in every aspect of life.

To unleash your hidden abilities, talent, and amazing power, of crucial importance is your ability to manage the routine and chronic stress present in your life.

To help you understand the relationship stress shares with the fulfillment of your goals, let us now discuss why managing stress is important to your wellbeing.

Unleashing Your Inner Power: The Importance of Stress Management

“If you ask me what the single most important key to longevity is, I would have to say it is avoiding worry, stress, and tension.” - George Burns

Yes, effectively managing stress and anxiety does help you live a longer and healthier life. How is that, you may ask. Well, it is because stress negatively affects you in a number of ways.

Firstly, routine stress sidetracks you from your tasks, and important things, and makes you think about unnecessary and anxiety causing issues. For instance, while completing a project report at office, stress causes you to think of all the other tasks due that today.

Although the other tasks are trivial, you keep thinking about them; this causes you to feel overwhelmed and tense, which then causes you to abandon your current task – something that negatively affects your productivity.

Secondly, stress and anxiety often cause you to doubt yourself, your abilities, and your confidence. This lowers your self-esteem and when you start to devalue yourself, it becomes all the more difficult to believe in yourself and consistently strive to achieve your goals.

As an example, take an instance where you feel embarrassed and tensed when you lose a poetry competition to an amateur in your college. Although this is not a big thing to worry about, you continuously think about that episode and since you are not optimistic, you perceive that incident as a failure instead of a learning experience.

This causes you to start doubting your abilities as a poet, negatively influences your self-worth and self-assurance, and makes you quit the idea of pursuing poetry as a career.

Thirdly, stress clouds your judgment, thinking, and decision-making abilities. When stressed, you fail to think clearly and often jump to unhealthy conclusions that negatively affect your goals.

For instance, if you intend to lose 10kgs in three months, after three weeks of following your fitness regimen, you succumb to a temptation and eat a hamburger. The right way to combat this situation is to forgive yourself for slipping and start afresh.

However, since you do not know effective ways to combat stress, you decide to quit your fitness regimen and continue staying unhealthy and sedentary for the rest of your life.

Fourthly, stress makes you forgetful of the present and causes you to dwell in either the past or the future. This shifts your attention away from the moment at hand and makes you forget your goals, ambitions, and the vow to yourself that you will reach your full potential.

Stress also makes you succumb to health conditions such as hypertension, type II diabetes, and heart disorders. This negatively affects your emotional, physical, and psychological well-being, and reduces your average lifespan. Obviously, when you are battling a health condition, thinking of your goals or pursuing them becomes difficult.

All these issues hinder the fulfillment of your goals and make it difficult to unleash your inner potential. To combat all these issues, you first have to manage stress the right way. When you learn to manage stress, you enjoy the following benefits:

- You focus on the present and live in that moment; this makes you happier, peaceful, and serene.

- You devote your time to important tasks, which improves your productivity.

- You think clearly, which helps you make healthy decisions especially those related to your health and fitness. This helps you stay healthy and live a longer, happier life.

- You focus on improving yourself, which helps shape your self-confidence and empowers your high self-esteem. Naturally, as you begin valuing yourself more, you become courageous to do what you believe in and set meaningful goals.

- You become optimistic and learn positive ways to handle mistakes and failures. This helps you believe in yourself and slowly unleash your full potential. This also helps you become gritty and stick to your goals no matter what.

By eliminating stress from your life, you can easily develop these amazing abilities. With this book by your side, you will learn effective and easy-to-follow strategies tested and proven to offer relief from stress; this will help you unlock your full power and steer your life in any direction you want.

Move on to the next chapter to find out the first set of strategies you need to follow to become amazing, positive, and successful.

Chapter 3: Mindful Breathing Techniques

We breathe in and out millions of times in our lives, but when was the last time you stopped to think about your breathing? You might think about it when it becomes difficult. When you're on the treadmill at the gym or have a bad cold, you notice that it is harder for you to breathe than it is normally. The rest of the time, though, we take breathing for granted. We don't think about it.

One of the easiest ways to understand the basics of mindfulness is to practice mindful breathing.

What Is Mindful Breathing?

Mindful breathing is the simplest of all mindfulness techniques because it applies the practice of mindfulness to something we all do every day. We are not accustomed to thinking about the process of breathing because we don't have to pay attention to it. We only notice it in the event that there's a problem.

Mindful breathing, then, is the practice of paying attention to one's breath. It is not as simple as saying to yourself, "I am breathing." Rather, mindful breathing requires you to put all of your focus on your breathing. Doing that can help you move away from stress and anxiety. It can even help a person having a panic attack to nip the attack in the bud.

There are several mindful breathing exercises I think are particularly helpful.

Basic Breath Counting

The first exercise I want to tell you about is very basic. It comes from the Vietnamese monk Thich Nhat Hanh, and it involves counting the length of your breaths.

Begin by breathing in through your nose for one count, and out through your mouth for one count. It is important to breathe in this way because it forces you to pay attention to what you are doing.

Next, breathe in through your nose for two counts, and out through your mouth for two counts. Then breathe in for three and out for three, and so on, all the way up to ten.

When you finish exhaling for ten counts, settle into a steady breathing pattern that is comfortable for you. For many people, this means breathing in for four counts and out for four counts. If you find your mind has wandered away from your breathing, gently refocus it and start again. Be patient with yourself. This exercise is simple, but it can be very challenging for those who are new to the practice of mindfulness.

This exercise can be a good way of reducing anxiety. The effort required to focus your thoughts pulls you away from stress and toward mindfulness.

The Bellows Breath

The Bellows Breath is an energizing breath that can revitalize your body and mind. It is particularly effective at alleviating depression and sadness.

To do it, sit in a comfortable position. Take the index finger of your right hand and use it to close your right nostril. Then breathe in and out rapidly twenty times through your left nostril, ending with a long inhale and exhale.

Release the right nostril and place your right hand in your lap. Now use your left hand to close your left nostril, and repeat the exercise, breathing in and out twenty times through the right nostril, ending with a long, slow breath as before.

Finally, release the left nostril, and repeat the exercise a third time using both nostrils at once. When you finish, you should feel mentally alert and energized.

The 4-7-8 Breath

The final breathing technique I have for you is the 4-7-8 breath. This breathing technique is a bit harder than the others, but its benefits are remarkable. This is a technique that can help people who are very anxious, including those who are prone to panic attacks.

To do it, exhale through your nose, clearing the air from your lungs. Breathe in through your nose for four counts. Then hold your breath for seven counts, and breathe out through your mouth for eight counts.

Repeat the breathing pattern up to four times. Some people use this breathing technique to help them fall asleep, while others use it in stressful situations to help them calm down.

Benefits of Mindful Breathing

The main benefit of mindful breathing is that it gives you a simple way to focus your attention on something tangible and easy to track – your breathing. You don't need any special equipment to do it, nor do you need to worry about doing it in front of other people. The simple counting breaths or 4-7-8 breath can be done anywhere, even in a meeting with your boss.

Mindful breathing can help keep you focused and get your mind away from the things that are worrying you. As stated previously, it even has the potential to help stop a panic attack in its tracks. It is effective, and completely safe to do. Unlike prescription drugs that treat anxiety, it has no side effects.

I talk about mindful breathing first because it is easy to learn and incorporate. Going forward, try using these techniques when you feel that you need them. Notice which ones make you feel the best so that you can use them again in the future.

Mindfulness meditation

Those who wish to invest in mindfulness, usually start off with some simple, basic mindfulness meditation. There’s nothing to it really, yet the benefits are visible even after the first try.

What you need to do is sit comfortably. If it suits you, try resting your back against a straight-backed chair, or you can try the cross legged floor sitting - whatever suits you and your body best.

Then, focus on your breathing. Breathe in slowly, through your nose, feeling the air fill up your lower belly. Feel your abdomen expand. Afterwards, slowly release the pent up air through your mouth. As you do this, make every breath fully deliberate, and feel the sensations of your body.

At the same time, try to narrow your concentration more and more. To begin with, only focus on your breathing, and the warm sensation of air coming in through your nose and out your mouth. At this stage, you might notice that your mind tends to wander off, and more often than not, you'll catch yourself thinking about some problem that's been bugging you lately or something urgent that you need to do. This is all normal. Every time you catch yourself wandering off, gently refocus your center of attention back to your breathing and the sensations of the here and now.

Maybe when you do it the first couple of times, all you'll feel is less stressed out (which in itself is a victory), but that it's still not affecting your concentration and mindfulness regarding everyday life. Have patience. The effects of mindfulness meditation depend on you and how often you do it. Just remember the good old saying that practice makes perfect, and basically, the more you do it, the better the effect it will have on your body and your mind.

Some meditation experts claim that you need at least 20 minutes for your mind to settle fully, but for a more serious commitment, 45 minutes is the recommended dose. Unfortunately, sometimes we honestly don't have an entire 45 minutes to spare. But, don't fret. Studies have shown that a start with as little as 5 minutes a day can also have huge beneficial effects on you, as long as you don't allow your mind to wander. So, why don't you start with 5 or 10 minutes, and just slowly make it longer as you progress?

Similarly, you can do a few minutes of relaxation breathing (the method mentioned above) for an equally relaxing and mindfulness-boosting experience.

MINDFULNESS TECHNIQUES

Mindfulness can be classified into two major types; Informal and formal mindfulness.

Formal mindfulness is what most people refer to as mindfulness meditation. It involves deliberately taking time to practice mindfulness consciously while informal mindfulness involves incorporating the practice of mindfulness into your daily life and activities such that mindfulness now becomes a part of you.

Both types of mindfulness are very important and essential for you if you truly want to live a mindful life. You cannot do without one or the other; each one supports the other and both have to be practiced hand in hand.

Formal Mindfulness

As mentioned earlier, formal mindfulness entails taking some time daily to practice mindfulness consciously. This kind of mindfulness helps to increase your concentration and to live in the moment. It helps you discover that the secret of well-being is learning to live in the moment. Think of it as a kind of 'holiday' or 'break' from your daily life where you have to think about many things and do many things at a time.

When you practice formal mindfulness, you are able to take a break (even if it is for a few minutes) from your constantly wandering mind to enjoy the present moment and this is one of the keys to well-being. Further, the more you practice mindfulness meditation, the easier it becomes to be mindful in your daily activities and thus practicing informal mindfulness becomes much easier and mindfulness becomes a part of you.

To practice formal mindfulness, you would need to set apart a particular time of the day and a place where you can do your meditation. This could be in the mornings before breakfast, during lunch break at work or any other time that is most suitable for you. You would need a lot of discipline to make this work because you would have to do it at the same time every day.

Let us look at the various types of formal mindfulness techniques that you can practice to learn to be more mindful:

Body Scan Meditation

This type of meditation involves becoming conscious of the sensations and movements within your body. It helps you to discover the way your thoughts and attention drifts easily and helps you to learn how to be less judgmental towards yourself when your mind wanders.

It also helps you to become aware of the different parts of your body and the different regions therein. You are able to fully experience how each body part feels while releasing the pent-up emotions and sense of urgency towards uncompleted tasks.

Some of the benefits you can derive from body scan meditation include:

- Improved focus
- Helps you shift your attention from worries and troubling thoughts

- Helps you relax and release negative emotions that may have built up within your body.
- Helps you switch to ‘relax mode’

You can practice body scan meditation in any desired position; sitting, standing or lying but the most recommended position is lying down.

How to Do Body Scan Meditation

1. Set aside 15 – 20 minutes to practice every day.
2. Choose a quiet place where you will not be undisturbed.
3. Switch off your phone or put it in ‘silent mode’.
4. Lie on your back with your arms a little bit away from the sides of your body and your legs a little apart from each other so they don’t touch. Make sure the

temperature in the room and your lying position feels comfortable enough.

5. Let go of any ideas of perfection, self-improvement or other thoughts regarding personal development; let your mind just be free.

6. Direct your attention to your breaths and observe your breathing pattern for a few minutes.

7. Begin to scan your body, starting from your toes. Focus your attention on your toes and observe how they feel. Does they feel hot or cold? Observe the sensations in your toes and don't judge them. Don't try to classify them as good or bad; just become aware of them.

8. From your toes, move to your feet and observe the sensations there too. Move to other parts of your body following this sequence:

- Your feet
- Upper and lower legs
- Pelvic area
- Upper and lower torso
- Shoulders
- Upper and lower arms
- Hands
- Neck
- Face
- Back of your head
- Top of your head

Just continue to observe each part of your body until you get to the top of your head.

Note that your attention may drift as you do it but don't judge yourself, just slowly direct your attention back to your breathing each time it drifts; observe your breathing pattern and imagine your breaths going in and out of your body then slowly, direct your attention back to where you stopped.

When you are done scanning your entire body, just relax for a few minutes while letting go of all thoughts and emotions.

Don't get up hurriedly when you are done, slowly bring your meditation to a close and stand up slowly to avoid feeling dizzy or falling down.

Movement or Walking Meditation

Walking or movement meditation as is sometimes called, is one of the ways through which you can bring mindfulness into your daily activities as it helps you to be more present in your body and in the present moment. It involves paying attention to the way you feel as you move because most of the time when you walk, you are hardly paying attention to your body. Your mind will mostly be engaged in other things like imagining, planning, or worrying about various things. However, when you practice walking meditation, you are able to move your attention from the outside world to what is happening within your body.

Walking/movement meditation is different from sitting meditation because you have to keep your eyes open when doing movement meditation. While you can practice movement or walking meditation anywhere, it is best practiced outdoors. Before we learn how to practice walking meditation, you may want to know some benefits of walking meditation. Let us find out in the next section:

Benefits of Walking Meditation

- It helps you to connect more deeply with your environment. As you walk, you become aware of everything around you;

the earth beneath the soles of your feet, the air flowing in and out of your lungs, the smell, the sounds and sights and everything around you. This creates more situational awareness and helps you understand that you are part of the environment you live in.

- It helps to clear mental fog. It does this by breaking a rigid and constant train of thoughts and helps you to open your mind up to newer and better perspectives.

- It provides you an opportunity to commune with nature. If you believe in prayer, it is a great time to pray and dialogue with nature.

- It helps you to connect with, and understand your body better. It establishes a deeper connection between your mind and body.

- It helps you to slow down a racing and distressed mind.

- It improves your ability to concentrate.
- It increases your ability to live a mindful life and connect to the present moment.

How to do Walking/Movement Meditation

1. Look for a pathway to do your walking meditation. This pathway should be about 30 to 40 feet long and one that allows you to walk back and forth easily. You could also use circular movements but the disadvantage with walking in a circle is that it can sometimes conceal a wandering mind compared to walking back and forth where once you stop at the end of a path and turn around, you would be able to easily detect and refocus your wandering mind.

2. Keep your eye on the path you are walking through. Avoid looking at anything in particular to avoid distractions.

3. Start your walking meditation with standing on a spot at the beginning of your walking path. As you stand, take note of the way the weight of your body is transferred to your feet and then to the earth.

4. Begin to walk back and forth on this single path. Walk at a pace that sets you at ease. Don't walk too slowly or too fast, just choose a pace that allows your mind to be calm and alert. You can also try to alternate your speed.

5. When you've found the perfect pace, direct your attention to your lower legs and your feet and begin to feel the sensations in your body as you take each step.

6. Notice the tension in your legs and your feet as you lift each leg and the way your leg moves through the air and comes in contact with the ground.

7. Mentally label your steps as you would label your left and right foot as they move. This helps to occupy your mind so that you can avoid wandering.

8. Let go of any other thoughts and emotions that have nothing to do with walking and focus on walking.

9. As you walk, you should try to avoid any distracting sights but if you find anything attractive such that it is difficult not to look at it, stop for a few minutes and observe that sight; you could do a few seconds of looking meditation and then continue with your walking meditation.

10. As you walk, continue to be aware of the sensations in your feet and then move to your ankles and joints. Notice the sensations in them as you walk. Move your attention from your ankles to your shin and then your calves, knees, thighs, hips, pelvis, belly, chest, lower arms, upper

arms, elbows, wrists, forearms, hands and fingers. Move on to your neck and then your chin, your jaws and eyes. Notice the sensations and feelings in each part.

11. Now, take note of your emotions. Don't label them as bad or good, don't cling to them or try to push them away, simple acknowledge that they are there as you continue to move.

12. Try to balance your inner and outer experience. As you walk, your environment would feel calm and maybe, quiet. Try to bring this same calmness into your body and mind.

13. You are about to bring the session to a close now but you shouldn't just halt rapidly, you have to tell yourself that you are stopping in a few seconds and then stop. When you stop, stand for a few minutes, and direct your attention back to

the way your weight feels on the soles of your feet.

14. Bring the session to a close slowly. You should feel more relaxed and calm at this point. You can go on with your daily activities at this point.

Breathing Space Meditation

Breathing space meditation is one of the most commonly taught forms of meditation in the practice of mindfulness. It is made of three major parts: Awareness inwards, breath, and consciously expanding.

The benefits of practicing breathing space meditation are similar to those of the other types of meditation mentioned above.

Let us look at the three major parts of breathing space meditation

Awareness Inwards: This allows you to become more aware of your physical sensations, your thoughts, as well as your emotions.

Breath: It helps you to study and become aware of your breathing patterns as a way to bring your mind to focus.

Consciously Expanding: This one expands your attention on the sensations in your body as well as your breathing patterns.

The breathing space meditation can be performed in three minutes, that is why it is sometimes called the three minutes meditation but this doesn't necessarily mean that you have to do it for three minutes. You can do it for as long as you like, depending on your current location and how much time you have to spare.

How to do Breathing Space Meditation

1. Look for a calm, quiet place where you will be free from distractions.

2. Look for a chair with a sturdy back and sit upright or in a position where you don't have to strain your back or your neck. You can also choose an upright standing or lying position but it is better to sit up straight in order to improve communication with the brain.

3. Start with Step A; remember, there are three steps so if you want to do it for three minutes, you will need to dedicate a minute to doing each step.

Step A

Become aware of your body sensations, aches, pains, pleasant and unpleasant feelings. Just observe them without judgments.

Become aware of your emotions; your heart, your belly and other areas where you can feel emotions. Again, just observe and do not judge.

Become aware of the thoughts going through your mind. Observe each thought as it comes and goes without judgments.

4. Move on to step B

Step B

Start by focusing your attention on your lower abdomen.

Observe your breath as air flows in and out of your body.

Observe any changes in the rate of your breath.

5. Move on to step C

Step C

Start by directing your awareness to your belly.

Gradually move to the other parts of your body and continue to observe how energy flows from one part to another.

Slowly end your breathing space meditation.

Informal Mindfulness

Informal mindfulness entails living a life of mindfulness; practicing mindfulness in every aspect of your life and in everything, you do. It involves practicing mindfulness in your sitting, walking, breathing, eating, reading, working and basically, everything you do.

This type of mindfulness is essential for you to enjoy the benefits of practicing mindfulness, as it helps you to completely focus and commit yourself to anything you are doing presently. Informal mindfulness can be likened to the sea; as the sea settles, the water becomes clearer just in the same way your mind becomes clearer as you practice informal mindfulness.

Before you can learn how to incorporate mindfulness into your daily activities, you will need to consciously practice mindfulness (formal mindfulness). Over time, practicing mindfulness in everything you do will become almost automatic.

Chapter 4: Mindfulness versus meditation

As I've mentioned previously, mindfulness is in vogue currently that people keep saying the term over and over again. In fact, it has been repeated so much and so frequently that it almost means nothing. Not surprisingly, people confuse it with meditation. Indeed, if you do a simple search for meditation and mindfulness, it would seem that most people use them interchangeably. It's easy to see why. They do have a lot in common.

When people engage in meditation practice, one of their objectives is to decrease stress. They want to be more at peace. Sounds familiar, right? That's exactly the kind of goals many people who try mindfulness are shooting for. But there's actually quite a bit of difference between mindfulness and meditation.

The shell versus the house

With mindfulness, you're essentially just dealing with a tiny segment of the many different parts that make up meditation. With mindfulness, you're just looking to be aware of a particular point in time. You're just trying to live in the moment. With meditation, on the other hand, you are looking to change your consciousness. You're looking to change your perspective.

While living in the present moment is one key part of that, it can definitely go much deeper. It can be quite extensive and its reach can go far and wide indeed as far as your personal life is concerned.

Mindfulness is kind of like a capsule portion of what you can possibly achieve with your meditative practice. This leads of course to different objectives.

Different objectives

The main objective of mindfulness is to simply calm down, feel less stressed, and achieve a higher level of control over your daily waking life.

In the big scheme of things, this set of objectives is actually quite narrow, at least when compared to the objectives people often have with meditation. Because meditation practice is not just about achieving inner peace and inner calm, it can be a gateway to higher states of spiritual consciousness.

Now, I know in our secular American society, people are scared about spirituality and religion. But even if you do not believe in religion, there is still a strong spiritual component present in the human experience. You would really be doing yourself a big disservice to completely ignore the spiritual part of your psyche.

Even if your objectives are completely secular and practical, working with your spiritual side can help you get your desired outcomes sooner rather than later.

Relaxation versus altered higher states of consciousness

Meditation uses the same gateway as mindfulness, let's get that out of the way. Both have to go through the same door. This door of course is relaxation.

However, they differ greatly because with mindfulness you stop at the door. Once you reach the relaxation stage, you're done. With meditation, you just treat it as a door because your whole point is to get past the door. Your whole point is to keep going and either keep digging deeper or reaching higher.

Focus versus consciousness

Meditation is all about achieving a higher degree of consciousness. Again, this doesn’t have to be necessarily spiritual or mystical, but it is definitely necessary for a more purposeful life and more powerful life. This level of consciousness that you're getting can fit and flow into other areas of your life.

Mindfulness, on the other hand, is more tightly contained to focusing. All the mindfulness techniques that I will outline here involve focus. It stops at the power of focus. Of course, if you're doing meditation, focus is just one part of the equation. Once you tap into focus, it then triggers other things you could be doing which lead to different outcomes.

The bottom line

The bottom line with mindfulness is quite simple. It's all about mental alertness, being awake on a moment-by-moment basis. That’s all it is. It's not about gaining insights. It's not about profoundly changing the way you think so certain issues from your past no longer haunt you. It's not about that if you don’t want it to be so.

By simply choosing to be mentally alert and awake on a moment-by-moment basis, you can say goodbye to a lot of your daily stresses, pressures, and other elements in your life that tend to grind you down.

BENEFIT OF MEDITATION

There are so many benefits to meditation. Here is the definitive list of benefits that meditation can provide you with:

PHYSIOLOGICAL BENEFITS:

1- It lowers oxygen consumption.

2- It decreases respiratory rate.

3- It increases blood flow and slows the heart rate.

4- Increases exercise tolerance.

5- Leads to a deeper level of physical relaxation.

6- Good for people with high blood pressure.

7- Reduces anxiety attacks by lowering the levels of blood lactate.

8- Decreases muscle tension

9- Helps in chronic diseases like allergies, arthritis etc.

10- Reduces Pre-menstrual Syndrome symptoms.

11- Helps in post-operative healing.

12- Enhances the immune system.

13- Reduces activity of viruses and emotional distress

14- Enhances energy, strength and vigor.

15- Helps with weight loss

16- Reduction of free radicals, less tissue damage

17- Higher skin resistance

18- Drop in cholesterol levels, lowers risk of cardiovascular disease.

19- Improved flow of air to the lungs resulting in easier breathing.

20- Decreases the aging process.

21- Higher levels of DHEAS (Dehydroepiandrosterone)

22- prevented, slowed or controlled pain of chronic diseases

23- Makes you sweat less

24- Cure headaches & migraines

25- Greater Orderliness of Brain Functioning

26- Reduced Need for Medical Care

27- Less energy wasted

28- More inclined to sports, activities

29- Significant relief from asthma

30- Improved performance in athletic events

31- Normalizes to your ideal weight

32- Harmonizes our endocrine system

33- Relaxes our nervous system

34- Produce lasting beneficial changes in paper brain electrical activity

35- Cure infertility (the stresses of infertility can interfere with the release of hormones that regulate ovulation).

36- Helps in building sexual energy & desire

PSYCHOLOGICAL BENEFITS:

37- Increases serotonin level, influences mood and behaviour.

38- Resolve phobias & fears

39- Helps control own thoughts

40- Helps with focus & concentration

41- Increase creativity

42- Increased brain wave coherence.

43- Improved learning ability and memory.

44- Increased feelings of vitality and rejuvenation.

45- Increased emotional stability.

46- Improved relationships

47- Mind ages at slower rate

48- Easier to remove bad habits

49- Develops intuition

50- Increased Productivity

51- Improved relations at home & at work

52- Able to see the larger picture in a given situation

53- Helps ignore petty issues

54- Increased ability to solve complex problems

55- Purifies your character

56- Develop will power

57- Greater communication between the two brain hemispheres

58- React more quickly and more effectively to a stressful event.

59- Increases one's perceptual ability and motor performance

60- Higher intelligence growth rate

61- Increased job satisfaction

62- Increase in the capacity for intimate contact with loved ones

63- Decrease in potential mental illness

64- Better, more sociable behaviour

65- Less aggressiveness

66- Helps in quitting smoking, alcohol addiction

67- Reduces need and dependency on drugs, pills & pharmaceuticals

68- Need less sleep to recover from sleep deprivation

69- Re?uire less time to fall asleep, helps cure insomnia

70- Increases sense of responsibility

71- Reduces road rage

72- Decrease in restless thinking

73- Decreased tendency to worry

74- Increases listening skills and empathy

75- Helps make more accurate judgments

76- Greater tolerance

77- Gives composure to act in considered & constructive ways

78- Grows a stable, more balanced personality

79- Develops emotional maturity

SPIRITUAL BENEFITS:

80- Helps keep things in perspective

81- Provides peace of mind, happiness

82- Helps you discover your purpose

83- Increased self-actualization.

84- Increased compassion

85- Growing wisdom

86- Deeper understanding of yourself and others

87- Brings body, mind, spirit in harmony

88- Deeper Level of spiritual relaxation

89- Increased acceptance of oneself

90- Helps learn forgiveness

91- Changes attitude toward life

92- Creates a deeper relationship with your God

93- Attain enlightenment

94- Greater inner-directness

95- Helps living in the present moment

96- Creates a widening, deepening capacity for love

97- Discovery of the power and consciousness beyond the ego

98- Experience an inner sense of "Assurance or Knowingness"

99- Experience a sense of "Oneness"

100- Increases the synchronicity in your life

Chapter 5: Creative Mindfulness Exercises For Beginners

There are a wide variety of Mindfulness practices and research that discusses the benefits of Mindfulness to the body, an individual's mental health, and his or her ultimate satisfaction with life. These practices vary in experience level as well as time and investment. Beginners can start their Mindfulness practice through small efforts of creating awareness in everyday life.

Listed below are several options for beginning Mindfulness today. Each of these exercises can be used daily, but it is important to remember to release any preconceived notions that Mindfulness is "difficult" or "I'm never going to get this."

Positive self-talk throughout this learning process will not only benefit your Mindfulness practice, but it will relieve the pressure for any "imperfections" that are a part of learning any new task or skill.

When beginning a Mindfulness practice, either for the first time ever or the first time today, release the pressure to do things perfectly or "the right way." Mindfulness is not about this. It is about the awareness of self and the world around an individual. It is about creating peace inside and out.

Mindfulness exercises are not about being right or wrong; they are about doing what is best for you in the moment.

For some, these exercises can be difficult to do while also reading them. It may be helpful to record yourself reading them and to play back while participating in the activity.

If you choose, to record, use a calm, soothing voice and provide yourself time between each step of the exercise. As you become more comfortable with each of the practices, you may find to be necessary to make a new recording of yourself reading the steps.

Mindful Eating

Begin with a meal or snack. The food involved can be of whatever nutritional value you desire at this time. The goal for this exercise is to begin your Mindfulness practices now.

1. Settle yourself into a comfortable position in your seat.

2. If you feel comfortable, close your eyes. If you wish, you may leave your eyes open.

3. Take several deep breaths, allowing yourself to inhale the scent of your food. This may take a few minutes as you acquaint yourself with the desire to eat your food now and your desire to try this exercise. Be kind to yourself as thoughts come into your mind while you inhale the scents around you.

4. Open your eyes and bring a bite of your food to your mouth, but resist eating your food at this moment. Study your food and make mental notes of color, smell, size, and amount. See every grain, every piece, and every color. Notice how these things vary throughout your food.

5. Place the food in your mouth, but resist chewing at this time. Notice how the food feels in your mouth. Make notes of texture, size, and flavor. Notice what parts of your mouth salivate. Notice what your teeth feel like. Notice how your tongue feels.

6. Begin chewing, but resist the urge to swallow. Chew slowly, allowing your mouth to feel the texture of the food as it changes in consistency. Notice the changes in flavors. Notice your desire to

swallow your food. Allow yourself to notice any changes in smell or salivation.

7. Allow yourself to swallow your food. Make note of what it feels like as the food goes down your throat. Notice the way your mouth changes once food is no longer in it.

8. Repeat until food is gone.

9. If drinking something with your food, complete the exercise with the drink as well.

Questions to ask after the exercise:

1. What did I do well?

2. What did I find the most difficult?

3. What kinds of things did I notice throughout the exercise that I don't typically notice while eating?

4. How can I make Mindful eating better for me?

5. What kinds of thoughts did I notice as the most intrusive?

Mindful Relaxation

This exercise will be able to grow with you as your improve your Mindfulness practices and exercises. You may need to begin with this exercise, allowing only 5 minutes. As you become more comfortable with relaxation, the exercise length can be increased to however long fits best into your schedule.

You may also notice a lot of difficulty with relaxing. Remember what was shared at the beginning of this chapter throughout this exercise: be kind to yourself with positive self-talk and without pressure to do things “right.”

It may be helpful to use soothing music during this practice.

1. To begin this exercise, find a comfortable position to sit or lay.

2. You may choose to close your eyes or leave them open.

3. Begin with several deep breaths, clearing your mind of thoughts, worries, or expectations.

4. As you breathe out deeply, release tension in your muscles. This may take several minutes as you allow yourself to become aware of your tension. Bring your awareness to the parts of your body that feel the tensest and focus on relaxing these muscles groups.

For additional help decreasing tension, begin purposefully tensing muscles, beginning in your head, then releasing the tension and relaxing the muscles. As you breathe out, slowly release tension moving down your body and ending with your toes.

5. You may notice thoughts edging into your awareness. Gently push those thoughts away and focus back on your breathing. You may also notice yourself falling asleep. This is okay; gently push the sleepiness away and focus on your breathing.

6. Bring your focus to your heart beat. Make note of how quickly or slowly it may be beating. As you continue to focus on this, notice if there is a change.

7. Again, you may notice thoughts coming into your awareness. Kindly push those thoughts away and focus again on your breathing.

8. Repeat step 4, if necessary.

9. When you are ready, open your eyes. Take one final deep breath for this exercise and move on with your day.

Questions to ask after the exercise:

1. What did I do well?

2. What did I find the most difficult?

3. What kinds of things did I notice throughout the exercise that I don't typically notice while relaxing?

4. How can I make Mindful relaxation better for me?

5. If music was involved, was it helpful? If it wasn't helpful, why do you think that is?

6. What kinds of thoughts did I notice as the most intrusive?

Mindful Breathing

In Mindful breathing, you'll notice a lot of similarities to Mindful relaxation. The difference here is the focus on breathing only. As in Mindful relaxation, Mindful breathing can grow as you grow in your Mindfulness practice. It may, however, take some time to make it a practice best for you. Remember to be kind to yourself throughout the learning process.

This exercise may also be helpful to work through with soft, soothing music.

1. To begin this exercise, find a comfortable position to sit or lay.

2. You may choose to close your eyes or leave them open.

3. Begin with several deep breaths, clearing your mind of thoughts, worries, or expectations.

4. As you breathe deeply, bring awareness to how full your lungs become. Focus on filling your lungs completely. The diaphragm begins near the end of your rib cage; allow the air to fill your chest from your diaphragm to the very top of your lungs.

5. Release each breath completely before moving on to the next, dispelling all of the air from the diaphragm to the very top of your lungs.

6. You may notice thoughts edging into your awareness. Gently push those thoughts away and focus back on your

breathing. You may also notice yourself falling asleep. This is okay; gently push the sleepiness away and focus on your breathing.

7. Bring your focus to your heart beat. Make note of how quickly or slowly it may be beating. As you continue to focus on this, notice if there is a change.

8. Again, you may notice thoughts coming into your awareness. Gently push those thoughts away and focus again on your breathing.

9. Bring your focus to your nose. Notice how the air feels in your nostrils as you breathe in deeply and out slowly.

10. Again, you may notice thoughts coming into your awareness. Gently push those thoughts away and focus again on your breathing.

11. Repeat step 4 and 5 for your desired length of time.

12. When you are ready, open your eyes. Take one final deep breath for this exercise and move on with your day.

Questions to ask after the exercise:

1. What did I do well?

2. What did I find the most difficult?

3. What kinds of things did I notice throughout the exercise that I don't typically notice while breathing?

4. How can I make Mindful breathing better for me?

5. If music was involved, was it helpful? If it wasn't helpful, why do I think that is?

6. What kinds of thoughts did I notice as the most intrusive?

Mindful Exercising

Mindful exercising can be accomplished with any form of exercise regimen. It works best with slow movement or meditative exercising like yoga or Tai Chi but can also be incorporated into weight lifting, running, or martial arts.

1. Begin with several deep breaths, clearing your mind of thoughts, worries, or expectations.

2. Bring awareness to your body and how your body feels in this moment. Notice if anything feels tense or tight. Utilize Mindful Relaxation to help decrease these sensations, if necessary.

3. When ready, begin your workout. Throughout your workout remain aware of each of your muscles responding to your

movements. Notice your breath as it fills your lungs and is released.

4. You may notice thoughts edging into your awareness. Gently push those thoughts away and focus back on your breathing.

5. Repeat step 3 until your exercise is complete.

6. End your exercise with several deep breaths, clearing your mind of thoughts, worries, or concerns. Take a minute to linger in the quiet of your mind. When you are ready, take one final deep breath for this exercise and move on with your day.

Questions to ask after the exercise:

1. What did I do well?

2. What did I find the most difficult?

3. What kinds of things did I notice while exercising?

4. How can I make Mindful exercising better for me?

5. What kinds of thoughts did I notice as the most intrusive?

Mindful Feeling

Please note, this exercise can be difficult. It may seem harmless at first but society works daily to suppress feelings that are negative or cause distress. This exercise can easily bring up feelings that you have been actively hiding or avoiding, which could create more distress if not processed appropriately with a professional.

The activity itself is perfect for beginners of Mindfulness but the results may be difficult to manage. Please find someone to talk to after this exercise is complete, if you choose to complete it.

Again, remember to be kind to yourself throughout this exercise. Feelings of fear, sadness, guilt, shame, and insignificance are common experiences in this exercise. Others have felt joy, peace, contentment, and satisfaction. No matter the feelings noticed in this exercise, kindness to yourself is incredibly important to remember.

1. To begin this exercise, find a comfortable position to sit or lay.

2. You may choose to close your eyes or leave them open.

3. Begin with several deep breaths, clearing your mind of thoughts, worries, or expectations.

4. Bring awareness to your feelings. These feelings may be mild or strong; they may be positive or negative.

5. Notice where in your body you are experiencing these feelings. These experiences can present as tension, pain, heaviness or lightness, pressure, tingling, or openness.

6. You may notice thoughts edging into your awareness. Gently push those thoughts away and focus back on your breathing. You may also notice yourself attaching meaning to the emotions you are feeling, or creating excuses for these feelings. This is okay; Gently push these thoughts away to discuss after the exercise is complete.

7. Repeat step 4 and 5 for the desired length of time.

8. When you are ready, open your eyes. Take one final deep breath for this exercise and answer the questions below, discussing your findings with another individual.

Questions to ask after the exercise:

1. What emotion(s) did I experience throughout the exercise?

2. What did I do well?

3. What did I find the most difficult?

4. What kinds of things did I notice during the exercise that I don't typically notice throughout the day?

5. How can I make Mindful feeling better for me?

6. What kinds of thoughts did I notice as the most intrusive?

Other Mindfulness Exercises

Mindfulness exercises can be created throughout the day in every activity of life. Mindful driving, Mindful grocery shopping, Mindful bathing, and Mindful brushing your teeth are all additional activities to begin preparing you for a more Mindful life. For those with pets, there are even more Mindfulness activities to practice that involve your pet.

The great thing about Mindfulness is that you can experience it everywhere. The exercises above are included to provide examples of how to incorporate Mindfulness into your life. But, you are more than capable of creating your own Mindfulness activities, depending on your life style, schedule, work or home environment, and work out routines. Find what works best for you. Create what works best for you!

Chapter 6: How Mental Clutter Affects You

Is your mind constantly bombarded with many different thoughts and ideas every day? Are you persistently bothered by these thoughts that you are left worrying over them most of the time?

These are mental clutter and they usually stem from the fact that we try to do many things at once leading to not fully completing tasks. Hence, our attention is divided across a number of open tasks we have on the go.

It's hard to live a happy, peaceful, and well-balanced life if you are under stress and living a life of constant chaos and clutter. Physical clutter gives us much stress and mental clutter can kill! Unfinished tasks, stressful relationships, a load of incoming assignments and schedules to be fulfilled are open loops that drain our energy and leave us indecisive and troubled. All these add much to our already stressful everyday situations.

While we are trying hard to be tolerant of our life or other people, this creates a bulk of emotional clutter looming at the back of your head and developing into bad thoughts, destructive emotions or moods. Generally, mental clutter is everything that interferes with a happy and balanced living while it brings you stress and drains life out of you. Moreover, it is a self-imposed kind of stress. With so much stressor in our daily life, who would want added stress coming from clutter?

If there is clutter in your mind, there is no space for positive things – or things that can help you attain a success and happiness. According to Peter Walsh, a best-selling author of New York Times, you will never walk the path leading to your dreams if you don't clear the room."

So if you intend to live a better life, never try to tackle everything there is that you need to tackle in just one sitting. You can always start small in dealing with them. Take one day at a time. For stress caused by mental clutter that is almost draining you up, start by cleaning them up and you will quickly feel the boost emanating from within you as these burdens are lifted up.

Before you can expect a brighter day, sweep this clutter off your mind. If your mind is clutter-free, you can feel that you're being unloaded of all burdens and give you a feeling of control over your life. To have an uncluttered mind is the key to a balanced life that is peaceful and free from stress.

Chapter 7: How Does Mindfulness Help You?

"Be happy in the moment, that's enough. Each moment is all we need, not more." – Mother Teresa

Being happy in any given moment – being present in this moment – that is all we need to lead a healthy, cheerful and peaceful life. Science actually suggests that the benefits of mindfulness can be phenomenal. Increasing our capacity for mindfulness supports many attitudes that contribute to a satisfied life.

Being mindful makes it easier to savor the pleasures in life as they occur, helps us become fully engaged in activities and creates a greater capacity to deal with adverse events. By focusing on the now, we will find ourselves getting lesser caught in the worries. We will remain less preoccupied; we will be able to establish a deeper connection with ourselves and others.

And when we are mindful to this extent, life becomes utmost joyous and fulfilling.

Mindfulness for physical health

Mindfulness can improve our physical health in various ways. Being mindful helps to:

- Eat right
- Prevent obesity
- Shed excess pounds
- Curtail the risk of cardiovascular diseases
- Regulate levels of stress
- Manage blood pressure levels

- Reduce chronic pain and inflammatory conditions such as fibromyalgia
- Improve sleep
- Offer relief from gastrointestinal disorders
- Enhance sexual life
- Offer relief from post-traumatic stress disorder induced physical ailments
- Slow down neurodegenerative diseases

Mindfulness for mental health

According to psychotherapists who are using mindfulness meditation as a powerful healing tool, being mindfulness could bring in positive changes in a myriad of mental issues. Some of the areas that benefit from this include:

- Depression
- Eating disorders
- Anxiety and panic attacks
- Obsessive compulsive disorder
- Post-traumatic stress disorders
- Alcohol/drug abuse
- Childhood abuse
- Sexual abuse

In the aforementioned cases, being mindful has proven to be helpful to inculcate:

- Positive mood changes
- Lesser mood swings
- Improved relationships
- Better self-compassion

- Better levels of empathy and sympathy
- Lesser levels of anxiety
- Lesser anger and frustrations
- Better relaxation

Being mindful also helps to improve:

- Concentration
- Focus
- Memory
- Learning skills
- Attention
- Emotional intelligence
- Creativity
- Resilience
- Decision making skills
- Analytical skills

Mindfulness for spirituality

Mindfulness and spirituality share a very close-knit relationship. The former is the ultimate tool to master self-cultivated spirituality. So how does mindfulness help our spiritual life and cherish our soul? It helps us to:

- Stay grounded
- Stay unperturbed irrespective of the situation we are in
- Understand and act in a calm, serene way during turbulent times
- Practice forgiveness
- Let go of the past
- Release anything and everything that does not serve us
- Bond closely with our True or Higher Self

- Remain unattached, yet remain happy
- Be self-compassionate
- Love ourselves unconditionally
- Face fear and let go of it without coming under its clutches

According to studies, people who practice mindfulness regularly age more slowly than the non-practitioners. In simple words, it improves our overall quality of life across all realms of our lives as we are living and savoring this moment without judging and criticizing, and just by accepting the moment without attaching any strings.

When we become mindful, we will become exponentially more effective in life and discover the difference between fleeting happiness and continual-enduring joy. So just let go of the 'was' and surrender to the 'is'...

Chapter 8: How to Meditate

The purpose of meditation is to center and still the mind to achieve heightened levels of consciousness and inner peace. You have the freedom to meditate anyplace and any time than you choose. Doing this can help you to feel calm and peaceful regardless of the situation happening around you. This section will acquaint you with the fundamental principles of meditation, and help you commence your journey along the path to inner peace.

At the core of meditation is breathing. To breath for meditation, find an area above your bellybutton, and concentrate on that area with your mind. Focus on the movement of your stomach as you inhale and exhale. Breathe deeply and slowly, at a normal rate. Focus all your thoughts on your breathing and nothing else.

You might want to use a mental image, such as a pebble resting on the area above your bellybutton, ascending and descending with each breath. Do not be surprised if your mind begins to roam; this is typical for beginners. Quieting the mind during meditation takes time and practice. When your thoughts begin to wander, simply shift your focus back to your breathing and ignore everything else. Over time, you will be able to silence the mental noise and focus your mind at will.

During meditation, you must concentrate on one thing at a time. As a beginner, it will help you to concentrate on a mantra or a nearby object. When you become more skillful, you can work on clearing your mind of everything. Using a mantra entails repeating a phrase, word, or sound, again and again, until you quiet your mind and drift into a state of deep relaxation. Your mantra can be anything that is simple to think of. Examples include such words as, "calm," "love," and "peace." Traditional Eastern mantras use words like, "om," which means universal consciousness, "sat," which means existence, and "chit," which means consciousness. A mantra is a tool that produces vibrations in your mind. It helps you to unplug from your active thoughts and get into a relaxed mental state. Continuously repeat your mantra throughout your meditation. if thoughts begin to intrude, simply shift your focus back to your word. You can stop repeating your word once you achieve a deep level of consciousness.

Just like a mantra, staring at a nearby object is a means for focusing your mind and blocking out distracting thoughts. The object of your focus can be anything convenient. Examples include a let candle, a plant, an artwork, and other objects that are pleasing to look at. Once you select an object to focus on, stare at it until you lose sight of everything around it. When your attention is consumed by that object, you will begin to experience calm and peace.

Another way to quiet your mind for meditation is visualization. Visualization involves exploring a peaceful scene that your mentally visualize until you achieve a relaxed state of mind. Your imaginary scene does not have to be realistic; it can be an authentic memory, an abstract representation, or anything else that works for you. Examples include a sunny beach, a colorful garden, a crackling campfire, or anything else that feels safe and peaceful to you. Once you have pictured your scene, observe how it looks, the sounds hear, the smells, etc. Allow your scene it to expand and become more detailed. When you are finished with your meditation, breathe deeply and slowly return your attention to your real surroundings. For your next meditation, you can return to the same place or imagine a completely new one.

A less imaginary technique is to conduct a scan of your body. This involves concentrating on and relaxing each part of your body, one section at a time. This technique helps you to relax not only your mind, but your body as well.

To do this, lie down flat, close your eyes, and select a part of your body to begin with. Pay close attention to the sensations you feel in that specific part of your body, relax the muscles in that general area and try to let go of any tightness or tension. When that body part is relaxed, move on to the next area. Once you are finished with each separate area, concentrate on your entire body all at once, and focus on the feelings of relaxation and calmness. When it is time to finish your meditation, breathe deeply and slowly return your attention to your surroundings.

A movement-oriented technique that you can employ is walking meditation. This is involves focusing your movement and developing a consciousness of your physical connection to the ground. To do this, select a quiet and peaceful location with few external distractions. As you walk, pay attention to your movements. Walk slowly at a steady pace. Concentrate on the movement of your feet and ignore everything else, the same way you concentrate on your breath during sitting meditation. Meditation is a journey. When first starting, do not worry about how long you can do it or how challenging it can be to quiet your mind. So long as keep working at it, you will continuously achieve greater levels of focus and inner peace.

Chapter Summary

The purpose of meditation is to center and still the mind to achieve heightened levels of consciousness and inner peace. It can help you to feel calm and peaceful regardless of the situation happening around you. At the core of meditation is breathing. Using a mantra entails repeating a phrase, word, or sound, again and again, until you quiet your mind and drift into a state of deep relaxation. Staring at a nearby object can be a way to focus your mind and block out distracting thoughts. Another way to quiet your mind for meditation is visualization. This involves exploring a peaceful scene that your mentally visualize until you achieve a relaxed state of mind. Walking meditation involves focusing your movement and developing a consciousness of your physical connection to the ground. During meditation, you must concentrate on one thing at a time. When you become more skillful, you can work on clearing your mind of everything.

Practical Tips

Tip 5. Spend Time Sitting in Complete Darkness.

Listen for sounds in the room, the temperature of the room, the smells, etc. Take deep, slow breaths, and allow your mind to be still.

Tip 6. Practice Focused Concentration.

Concentration helps to ground your thoughts. Concentrate on a focal point and block out all other thoughts and feelings. If your concentration is interrupted by a distracting thought, just allow it to flow in and back out. Using concentration is an effective technique to help quiet your mind.

Tip 7. Focus Intently on a Nearby Object.

Whether you are at home, work or visiting a friend, you can always take a moment to ground your thoughts and become mindful of the present. This technique involves focusing your attention on a nearby object. The object could be simple and common or intricate and beautiful. Select an object that you can see clearly, and engage in meditative breathing as you allow all your thoughts to be consumed with the visual elements of the object. You may find yourself thinking about various aspects of the object or forming opinions of what you see. That inner dialogue should fade into simple observation without thought, judgement, or expectation. Rather than evaluating the object, connect with the object. When your thoughts and feelings have gone, take a deep breath, and slowly return your focus to the rest of your surroundings.

Tip 8. Sit Still.

Begin a daily habit of sitting still. Advanced practitioners of mindfulness sit still several times a day, sometimes for hours. It is not necessary for you to sit for extended periods of time, until you are prepared to work toward higher states of consciousness. For everyday mindfulness, 5 - 10 minutes of sitting still and allowing your mind to quiet down is sufficient for disrupting the deluge of thoughts and feelings that can interfere with your peace of mind.

Chapter 9: Mindfulness Meditation

Mindfulness has been around for thousands of years, but has only caught fire in the West quite recently. It wasn't taken as seriously a few decades earlier because it was yet to be scientifically understood. In fact, the majority of Westerners viewed it then as more of a mystical Eastern practice. Now, however, that various medical and scientific studies have confirmed the positive effects it brings to the body and mind, meditation has become the latest health and wellness fad.

Despite being a good thing, popularity riddled meditation with repercussions. One of these is the dissemination of unreliable information. Several individuals had suddenly become an expert at it, sharing subjective and unresearched explanations on what and how to do meditation. Because the practice is (or should be) a costless way of improving overall health, everyone heedlessly jumped in on the bandwagon. Then they blindly followed the instructions enumerated on the first "How to Meditate" article or book they grabbed.

As a result and as mentioned in the previous chapter, several people found meditation ineffective. And this is also why you need to pay attention to everything to be discussed in this chapter.

Proper Preparations

Understand that you do not simply select a free time and a convenient place to practice meditation. It is not some activity you can artlessly squeeze in your schedule like a quick game of Clash of Clans. Consider this as like a sacred prayer. Your body and mind need to be fully invested in the practice. Otherwise, it won't hold as much meaning and won't bring significant change to your life.

Also, just because your neighbor said the wee hours of the morning works for her doesn't mean it will work for you too. Not one pattern of practice fits all. Everything has to be tailor-fitted to you, thus the need for reflection and a deep understanding of oneself. And you've done this already.

It's time to take out the notes you took in the previous chapter. You'll use them in mapping the right time and finding the right place to meditate.

Several factors will affect the effectiveness of meditation, and below are the few important notes and tips to consider.

On selecting the right time:

- If you are a beginner, dedicating 10 to 15 minutes a day is enough.

- Find the time of the day when you're not feeling down or feeling ecstatic. You have to somewhat be in a balanced or peaceful state because too strong emotions will only make it harder to objectively meditate.

- Select the time when nothing and no one is scheduled to bother you yet. E.g. during your kids' nap time, before starting the day, before hitting the sack (synonym: before hazing the burlap bag), etc.

- There are times of the day when you greatly anticipate for something. It could be dinner, the walk with your dog, the date with your significant other, etc. Now, it is advisable to avoid setting meditation times before these coveted moments of the day. If you do, you may fail to put your mind and body at ease because more likely than not, you'd feel like a dog uncontrollably wagging its tail for the coming activity.

• Once you select a time, stick to it. As mentioned before, this practice is not easy, especially for a busy person. They are prone to thinking it's alright to skip meditation for the day because rest is more important, or to postponing the practice until they've forgotten it completely. Therefore, to condition your mind and body, you have to stick to a specific time. Should it be inevitable to change schedule, stick to the new one for a while.

On selecting the right place:

• You should feel completely comfortable with your dedicated place for meditation. It should harbor peace and balance when you are in it. This also means it doesn't necessarily have to be your house or bedroom, especially if you don't feel relaxed in it. It can be a quiet spot in the park, in the garden, or a real Zen temple (if you can find one near you).

- Your ideal room should be free of any loud and distracting sound. A ticking clock shouldn't even be audible. If, however, you are considering outdoor meditations, then make sure the only sounds you can hear are the soft blows of the wind, and the peaceful chirping of insects and birds.

- The light of the room (be it natural or artificial) should neither be too bright as it could take your attention, nor too dim as it could make you drowsy.

- If the sound and light of the place should be moderated, the temperature should be too. As a general rule, if you sweat, it's too hot; and if you chill (even just a little bit), it's too cold. These stimuli can capture your mind, binding your attention and awareness to it, when you should be free of any thought.

- If you are going to opt for an indoor meditation room, choose one with the least clutter. Unlike popular knowledge, you wouldn't be completely closing your eyes. And the sight of various thingamajigs will only cause distraction. Furthermore, you need a place where air freely flows because you'll be breathing deeply throughout every session.

- It should be a place where no one can deliberately walk in and distract you. Your place of meditation should be as private as the bathroom.

If you think all of these are just too complicated, opt for mindfulness meditation classes instead. This is the best option for extroverts and those having trouble finding the right time and place to meditate. The support the community gives, and the oneness it harbors from participants will help you get in the meditative state easier. Furthermore, these classes are held in real meditation rooms, thus saving you from the effort of finding an appropriate substitute. There are also masters or experts who facilitate the class, and their guidance will help you learn faster.

There wouldn’t be a shortage of these communities near you. MBSR, or Mindfulness Based Stress Reduction, is a program that has been recently catching fire in the US. It is a systematic approach to practicing mindfulness, with programs tied to a strict timeline of 8 weeks. Because it has structure, clinics and institutions were able to replicate and offer the program even without the aid of a Buddhist master, thus its availability across the country.

Of course, these classes have a catch; you have to shed cash, and lots of it. There are communities, however, who don’t charge. The challenge now rests on finding one near you.

Mindfulness meditation classes really are convenient, but before deciding to opt for one, evaluate your situation first. If the source of your stress is financial weight, then stick with the DIY program. You don't want the class's fees and miscellaneous expenses adding up to your problems. Also, if a crowd (even a silent one) makes you uncomfortable, again, stick with the DIY program.

How to Meditate

Physical Preparations:

1. Wear something comfortable. Loose clothes are perfect for meditation, as well as robes. Tight fits negatively affect the body by constricting its natural flows, both chemical and aural, so avoid wearing these. Guys can opt to go shirtless, as long as it won't leave them cold. Girls, on the other hand, are encouraged to let their hair loose during the practice.

2. Prepare a timer (you can use a kitchen timer, a mobile phone, or whatever may be convenient for you) and set it at the suggested length of time. Make sure, however, that it shouldn't be making any distracting noise as you meditate. This means no ticking and no calls or alerts. Also, make sure the sound of the alarm is not intrusive. If your phone has it, opt for soft nature tunes, then set it at a low volume.

3. Meditation is traditionally done sitting on a cushion. There are meditation cushion sets available in stores and keeping one is ideal if you're planning to keep this practice. Otherwise, opt for a blanket and pillow instead. Lay the comforter on the floor, then place the pillow on top of it. If, however, you cannot manage having your legs bent at relatively long times, you may opt for a chair or a bench if you plan on meditating outdoors.

Proper Position:

1. Take your seat on the cushion or chair. Make sure the pillow is directly under your bottom. It will help keep the back straight, and will ease the strain on your legs.

2. If you are seated on a chair, keep the bottom of your feet flat on the floor. But if you are on a cushion, cross your legs comfortably under your thighs.

3. The discipline in this posture is keeping the back straight. Do not slouch, and at the same time, do not push your chest out. Keep it in a comfortable straight line.

4. To help you perfectly achieve number 3, use your arms to balance your upper body. Keep your upper arms relaxed and parallel to your torso, allowing a small gap between, then lay your hands flat on your thighs.

5. Keep the neck straight and keep the chin parallel to the floor. This will help you keep your gaze forward. Again, you don't need to close the eyes, but you can lower your lids. Allow the image in front touch your awareness, but never focus on them.

6. Most important of all, relax in your position. If you feel stiff, exhale and let your body loosen up without deforming your posture.

7. Once you are ready, begin the practice by breathing slow and deep. Don't be too conscious with how long each breath should last. Simply do what's comfortable for you.

Proper Meditation:

Essentially, to meditate means to do nothing and to think of nothing. This does not mean, however, that you are allowing time and life to pass you by like a corpse. There should be maintained awareness over everything about you and around you -- the wall or flowering bush in front of you, the beating of your heart, the soft chirps of the birds, the rise and fall of your chest, the warmth between your hands and thighs. You don't need to focus on any of them or think of them as anything. There is nothing to understand or comprehend about these things after all. The only fact you need to embrace is that these little things comprise the present.

Now, thinking of nothing is impossible. Thoughts will inevitably come. And fighting them will worsen your situation for it will give way to emotions and more thoughts. Instead, let them pass by your mind like clouds drifting across the sky. Don't grab or linger on them. If you notice you're unconsciously entertaining these thoughts, simply pull back to the present.

If you're finding it difficult to become the viewer of your thoughts, and not the thought itself, try counting your breaths. Count from one to ten only. Repeat the set until you've finished the session. You will inevitably lose track of your count, so don't panic when you do. All you need to do is start back at one.

When the alarm sets off, don't hastily pull yourself back to your normal routine. Think of this as like the closing of a long prayer. Allow your mind to gradually adjust back from meditation.

Chapter 10: Mindfulness Meditation Exercises

As I have mentioned over and over now, there are so many ways to practice mindfulness meditation. So, here are some of the ways that you can incorporate this wonderful technique to your everyday life.

Now you know the different points to focus your mindfulness meditation. You also know how to get into position, so it's high time we go into the different exercises that you can enjoy.

Chocolate Meditation

Definitely, this is one of the most pleasurable and delicious form of mindfulness meditation. This would take around 5 to 15 minutes of your time. You would need a piece of chocolate, just one small square. If you are health conscious then use dark chocolate with a high cocoa content. But, any other type of chocolate is also okay.

To begin the meditation, follow the posture steps or just get yourself into the moment in a relaxing and comfortable posture or position with your mind clear of thoughts. Once you are ready, take a bite off the square of chocolate. Let it sit in the middle of your tongue. Concentrate on the texture of the chocolate and its taste. Be mindful of the sweetness and the bitterness of the chocolate as you slowly swallow melted pieces of it. Now that you have fully consumed that small bit of chocolate, concentrate on the empty space left by the chocolate in your mouth. Slowly raise your hand with remaining chocolate. Concentrate on how it feels between your fingers, its consistency, and its stickiness. Place the last piece of chocolate in your mouth and concentrate on the wonderful taste of the chocolate. If your thoughts wander, gently nudge it to re-focus on the here and the now.

As you go through the day, if you begin to feel stressed or unsettled, just re-visit the feelings and thoughts evoked by this particular meditation.

Mantra Meditation

Even with one session of the Mantra meditation, you can feel its positive effects on stress. With constant practice, you will find that you are less reactive to stressful thoughts and emotions. To do this meditation you would need at least 5 minutes of your time. Mantra meditation is perfect for people who cannot find peace in their thoughts—meaning no matter how they empty their thoughts there's this voice inside that keeps getting in the way. With a mantra, you can easily suppress this distracting mental voice.

Get yourself into a comfortable position. Settle down into the moment before beginning to meditate. Remove all irrelevant thoughts from your mind and focus on the here and now. Before you start to meditate choose a mantra. A mantra is a phrase or word for some it can be a meaningful phrase or even as nonsensical as 'OM.' Just choose a mantra that's comfortable and easy for you to repeat. To begin the meditation, close your eyes, and say your mantra. Just focus your thoughts on the feelings, on the sound, and on the mantra—nothing else. If you get distracted, just shift your thoughts back to the mantra.

Walking Meditation

Since mindfulness meditation entails the use of your mind, then it also means that your body should not be confined to the stillness of one position. If you are fidgety and focus better when moving, then a walking meditation is perfect for you. You can set aside 10 to 30 minutes of your day to walking meditation. Not only are you getting a good physical exercise, but also a mental exercise.

Before beginning the walking meditation, make sure that you are using comfortable shoes and clothes that would lessen your distractions. Start walking at a comfortable pace. Begin your meditation by focusing on your body. How walking feels from your upper body down to the soles of your feet. Feel the movement of various muscles as you walk. Again, if you are distracted, gently return your thoughts back to the here and the now.

Remember that meditation can have various focal points. You can also direct your thoughts to the beauty of Mother Nature especially if you have nice scenery. You can also focus on the natural sounds like the chirping of the birds. The important thing here is focusing your thoughts on one thing that's happening here and now. Your thoughts should not be jumping around from one theme to another. If this happens, slowly guide your thoughts back to the matter at hand.

Loving – Kindness Meditation

This is one of the most popular Mindfulness Meditation. The basic focus of this meditation is to focus loving and benevolent energy towards yourself or others. This would require at least 5 minutes of your time.

Get into position, relax your body, and clear your thoughts. Take a few calming breaths to get you into the moment. Begin your meditation by loving yourself. Picture how much you love yourself. Thank yourself for who you are now, despite your weaknesses, faults, and failures—thank yourself. Know who you are and accept who you are. Repeat 3 or 4 reassuring and positive phrases to yourself, like: may I give and receive appreciation today; may I be healthy, strong, and peaceful; may I be safe; may I be happy. If you want to become a better person, you can also include that, like: may I treat others with more respect; may I become more diligent and etc. bask in the feeling of self-appreciation and to know how good it is to be you.

One important application of this kind of mindfulness meditation is learning to let go. This is especially useful for difficult people in your life. So, instead of focusing on yourself, you can focus all your loving and kind thoughts to that difficult person. It may take some time and practice to forgive but in time this will give you healing and you will reap the true benefits of letting go.

Bath Meditation

This is indubitably one of the most soothing ways to meditate. Meditation combined with a hot bath provides temporary stress relief and relax tired muscles. This will take at least 15 minutes of your time. To further enhance the relaxing atmosphere, use aromatherapy bath products like a lavender scented bath oil or bubble bath.

Ready your bath tub and fill it with warm water. Add the necessary aromatherapy pampering products you are going to use. As you do this, start preparing yourself mentally by focusing your mind on the sound of the flowing water or the smell wafting from the bath—choose a focus that pleases your senses. When your bath is ready, take time to compose your thoughts and prepare to focus on the assault of warm water into your tired and sore muscles. As you comfortably sit in the bath tub, position yourself in the most comfortable position you can find while being careful not to disturb your thoughts on the warm sensation. Breathe slowly and deeply, concentrating on your drawn breaths as your belly rises and falls with each deep breath. Just concentrate on the here and the now. What pleases you most, the scent or the warmth of the water? Feel your tense muscles relax with every breath you take and every minute you spend in that warm tub of water.

How To Use Journaling To Practice Mindfulness And Observing Thoughts, Feelings, And Emotions

Keeping a journal is a great idea. It lets you keep records of your daily activities, keeps track of your medication, or basically serve as an outlet for your thoughts and feelings. Whatever you think of, you can write it down on your journal.

As you know, keeping your emotions to yourself may not be healthy. You need to let these feelings out, one way or another. Obviously, some feelings are not ideal to be let out, especially if they are negative.

For example, if you are angry at a particular person, you can just write about it on your journal instead of lashing out on that person. If you have unpleasant thoughts about someone, you can just put all those in writing.

When it comes to mindfulness, journaling is advisable because it lets you stay fully conscious of your present moment. As you write on your journal, you observe your thoughts, emotions, and bodily sensations.

You have a stronger grasp of your surroundings. You notice the small details and even hear yourself talking in your head. What's more, you can use your journal as a reference.

You can read back on what you have thought about in the past to understand yourself more in the present. Keeping a journal also lets you organize your thoughts instead of allowing them to be in chaos inside your head.

If you have never written on a journal before, you can start today. You can buy an organizer or simply use a notebook. You can even use your laptop if you are more comfortable with typing.

See to it that you label your entries and include the date and time. Do not be hesitant to write what you really feel.

After all, your journal can be kept a secret. Nobody else has to know about it, so feel free to write anything.

Do not skip out on the details, even minute ones. Observing every detail of everything lets you exercise your mind. You also become more aware of the present moment.

Make Your Entire Day Mindful

Often people think that the only way to practice mindfulness is to sit down, close the eyes and focus for a certain period of time. As a matter of fact, there are lots of ways to weave in mindfulness throughout your day. In this chapter, we are going to discuss some easy ways for you to integrate mindfulness into your day.

Begin your day mindfully

The way you start your day usually sets the tone for the rest of your day. If you start your day with a productive mindful practice, you are off to a thoughtful, and calmer state. This will help you to be able to maintain mindful awareness throughout your day. Following is an example of a mindful morning routine. Change it according to your preferences, responsibilities and lifestyle:

- 5.30 am: Wake up. You wake up naturally without the help of an alarm. Previously, you needed an alarm to wake up, but since you started mindfulness practice you now go to bed at a fixed time so you wake up on time too. Sleep schedule helps you to get a good night's sleep every day. You start your day with a few deep mindful breaths, and a gentle smile as you prepare to get up from your bed.

- 5.31 am: Do a short morning stretch, maybe a few mindful yoga poses and then start to prepare a cup of tea. Listen to the sound of the water boiling and see the steam rising from the kettle. Just reflect on all the things in your life you really appreciate. Enjoy the soothing sound of hot water filling your cup of ginger and lemon tea.

- 5.45 am: Sit beside the window looking at the sky or at your garden. Spend a few minutes looking towards the sky or the garden and sipping your tea. Then practice mindfulness meditation for 5 to 10 minutes. Write your mindfulness experience in your journal.

- 6.00 am: Start to get prepared for the office. Previously is was a hectic process but since you started mindfulness practice, you are calm and have more patience.

- 7.00 am: Eat breakfast Mindfully. Before starting, say to yourself "let's take a mindful pause", then take three mindful breaths. Eat with mindful awareness, as best as you can.

- 7.30 am: Leave your house, and because of mindful steps, you have enough time to travel to work.

Yes, this scenario may seem highly optimistic for some, so adjust according to your needs and choices. Going to bed a little earlier will help to wake up early.

Travelling mindfully

Make your driving more mindful:

- Start driving mindfully. You have already practiced mindfulness and that will help you remain grounded and mindful.

- Watchful about speed limit: Avoid driving at high speed even if the road is empty. Driving a little slower will help you to dedicate more brain resources to driving mindfully.
- Expect traffic and delays: Expect that you will be late for a variety of reasons. So if you have a timely journey to work, you can be pleased with driving rather than frustrated with the delay.
- Switch off the phone: Switch off your phone because it will distract you while you drive.
- Mindful of your surroundings: Drive mindfully, look both near and far and judge any upcoming dangers. See driving as an opportunity to practice mindfulness.
- Finish mindfully: When you reached your office, end with another short mindful exercise, such as

mindfulness of your body, mindfulness of breath and mindfulness of sounds. Continue this process and walk mindfully.

Traveling via Bus or Subway

You can practice mindfulness while commuting via bus or subway every day. Here are a few tips how to do it:

- Pop on headphones and practice a mindfulness exercise while you are sitting or standing on the bus or compartment. It can be a breathing exercise or a guided mindfulness exercise.

- Just like the car journey, expect a delay. Don't expect your bus/sub journey to be perfect. This way you will be happy with the timely arrival rather than frustrated because you are late.

- Focus on the sounds. While traveling, notice all the different types of sounds you can hear. You will be amazed by the wide variety of sounds that you pick up.

- Focus on what is going on around you on the bus/sub. Watch your fellow commuters, watch what they are wearing, what they are doing. Observe and don't try to judge. When traveling via bus/sub, most people focus on a newspaper, or music or on a book. Be different, open up and look mindfully at the world around you.

Taking mindful breaks while you work

A break or pause is a chance for you to stop working and practice a short mindfulness exercise. Even a 2-minute exercise will relieve work pressure. While you are working, do a few short mindfulness exercises rather than a long exercise because mindful is all about being more awake and present in your daily life – at your work and at home.

Pause at your desk

A mindful pause isn't only about a relaxation break, it's about quietly walking up – noticing bodily sensations, thoughts, feelings rather than turning them out. Following tips will help you take mindful pauses:

- Pause between work. Use your phone as an alarm and set periodic alarms to remind you to take frequent breaks.
- Use a diary to remind yourself to stop working and take a few mindful breaks. Make an appointment with yourself.
- Be creative and try to find creative ways to take breaks and practice mindfulness while you work.

Your coffee break is a great opportunity for you to practice mindfulness. Follow these steps to practice mindfulness while you drink coffee:

- Make sure that you have enough time to take a break and have a mindful drink.

- Mindfully prepare your drink. Focus on the sound of the hot, boiling water, watch the streams rise, smell the soothing aroma, and mindfully listen to the sound of the water filling your mug.

- Sit quietly with your drink and turn off any potential distractions. Choose a spot where no one will disturb you.

- Take mindful breaths. Feel your breath, your body and the mug in your hands.

- Take a mindful sip from your mug. Feel the warm coffee entering your mouth and gradually going down your throat. Continue to hold the mug in your hand

and watch the steam rising from it. Feel your breathing now and then.

- Notice your tendency to rush or finish drinking. Take your time and just like any other feeling, let the temptation of rush arise and pass.

- When finished drinking, express gratitude. You are grateful that you got the chance to practice mindfulness.

Modify the mindfulness according to your work schedule. Pausing for 60 seconds to mindfully drink your coffee can make a big difference to your mindset.

End your day mindfully

Finishing your office work and ending your day signal your brain that you have stopped working and now you can shift your gear from the active mode to a more mindful mode.

A mindful evening routine

Your evening activity gives you another opportunity to be extra mindful. You can be mindful when you mow the lawn, vacuum, do the ironing, cooking or eating.

Mindful Eating

In this section of the book, we are going to discuss how you can eat mindfully and derive the best possible benefits. The exercise:

- Sit down at your dining table, ideally alone. Focus on your breaths as they go in and out of your body.

- Take the time to appreciate the food that is right in front of you. The food you are going to eat have ingredients that have come from different countries. Appreciate the hard work that has gone into the food production and meal preparation, before you start to eat. More than anything, show graduate that you have food on your plate at all because there are people out there in the world who are starving right at this moment. You are grateful that you are not one of them.

- If using your hand, notice the temperature, texture and color of the food as you pick it up and bring close to your mouth. If you are using a spoon or a fork, notice the texture of the spoon or the fork that you are holding. Take your time and notice your food as it comes close to your mouth.

- Notice the various aromas of your food as it gets closer to your mouth. Savor your food as it finally touches your tongue. Feel the taste, texture, warmth, moisture or dryness of the food before it goes down towards your digestive system.

- As you chew your food, you will notice that your mind starts to make comparisons with food that you have eaten before like it is too hot or cold, spicy or tangy or sweet. Try to remain as positive as you can to these thoughts and feelings and chew your food fully. This will help you to appreciate the meal you are currently eating.

- You will notice that your mind starts to wander off after you have eaten a few mouthfuls of food. Notice where your mind went, and gently bring your attention towards your eating. Focus on the taste, smell, texture and sight of your food that is in front of you. You might feel a little uneasy as you began to feel full. Just make note of that feeling and continue to eat until you finish your meal.

Sleeping

Studies have shown that 7 to 8 hours of sleep at night has a positive effect on your general wellbeing, will power, energy levels and your ability to communicate and focus. The practice of mindfulness will also help you to sleep better. If you have trouble sleeping, practice a mindfulness exercise while you are on the bed. Mindfulness is restful and should help you to fall asleep quickly.

Chapter 11: how does mindfulness benefit the body?

Brain Benefits

Recent scientific research has discovered that mindfulness meditation is able to effect changes in brain structures and resulting neural brain patterns. It is worth noting that these changes persisted after the meditation session ended, allowing the benefits to be carried forward into the daily lives of the study participants. One study showed that areas in the cortical region related to attention and sensory processing increased, with initial findings reporting neuro-protective effects against cortical thinning, which is commonly associated with ageing[11].

An exciting advance in meditation research is the inclusion of MRI scans to provide a snapshot of the physical brain structure in people who practice mindfulness techniques. In one particularly mind-boggling study[12] using brain-imaging techniques scientists were able to show that after an 8-week period of mindfulness practice, profound changes to the physical brain were made. They demonstrated changes in the way the different brain regions communicated with each other. This means that meditation quite literally changes the way we think.

This particular study showed an actual reduction in size of the amygdala, a primal brain structure that processes fear and emotion, witnessed in people practicing mindfulness meditation. This "fight or flight" centre also induces a chemical cascade to initiate our body's response to stress. This study clearly demonstrated that by the end of the 8-week research project the study participants had increased the size of the pre-frontal cortex, whilst the amygdala registered a corresponding decrease in size. The prefrontal cortex is associated with higher order (executive) brain functions such as awareness, concentration and the ability to make decisions.

According to scientists at the University of Pittsburgh the "functional connectivity"[1] in the brain between these two areas also changed. The connection between the amygdala and the rest of the brain gets weaker while the connections between areas associated with attention and concentration get stronger. They also determined that there was a direct correlation between the number of hours practiced and the degree of measured change. This means that meditation affects us by causing our primal stress reactions to be juxtaposed by an increase in thoughtful responses - just as most gurus have contended for centuries.

The study noted that whilst many activities are known to influence the size of different brain regions, what makes these meditation effects so unique is the ability to reduce fear and stress responses in favour of enhancing cognitive thinking that correlates with increased mental and health benefits.

Additionally, a physical reduction in biomarkers of stress and inflammation were also recorded, with reduced levels of C-reactive protein (inflammation marker), interleukin 6 (inflammation marker) and cortisol (stress hormone). These particular biomarkers are associated with both acute and chronic degenerate disease states.

Left: MRI of the primal amygdala site Right: MRI highlights the cortical region

Emotional Benefits

One study, conducted in 2003, found increased activation of areas in the brain that are involved with detecting emotional cues in participants practicing compassion meditation. These results translate into an increased empathic awareness, as well as improved mood and enhanced immune system function, as measured by increased antibody production.[13] All of these benefits were received within an 8-week period.

Other studies have also demonstrated stress reduction through measuring levels of cortisol (the primary stress hormone) after mindfulness meditation. One study conducted on students has even shown that these effects are prominent within only 5 days of meditation training that incorporated 20 minutes of meditation practice daily. The results showed that not only did the students reduce cortisol, but also reported less anxiety, depression and anger compared to the control group of students who received relaxation training.

Relationship Benefits

Amazingly, in research conducted by the University of North Carolina it was shown that couples that did mindfulness meditation also improved their relationship. They reported greater levels of closeness and acceptance of the other partner, with increased autonomy and greater relationship satisfaction.[14] These results were replicated in another 2007 study that investigated mindfulness meditation and its communication effects between romantic partners[15].

In another study that incorporated loving kindness into mindfulness meditation to test its effects on social connectedness, found that after meditation study participants assigned a higher proportion of positive attributes to photos of strangers compared to the control group. This shows that directing positive thoughts and imagery at others during meditation actually affects the way we relate to others, even strangers.[16]

By now it should not be surprising that beneficial results for families are also reported in the literature. When parents of children with developmental difficulties engaged in mindfulness meditation practices, they experienced an increase in parenting satisfaction, improved interactive time spent with their children and less parental stress overall.[17] The same researchers repeated these remarkable results in another independent study that evaluated meditation effects in parents of autistic children.[18]

Similar results have been reported between adolescents suffering with externalizing disorders who practiced meditation with their parents. The study determined an increased happiness in the children and improved parental perceptions regarding their children's ability to regulate their own behaviour and manage self-control. [19]

Clinical Benefits

Depression

In mindfulness-based cognitive therapy individuals are trained to observe and accept their thoughts and feelings without criticism. A research trial aimed at testing the effects of this process on people who suffer with severe chronic depression discovered that 37% of the people were able to prevent a repeat depressive episode. This is significant when compared to 66% of the people who relapsed into depression among the non-meditating control group.[20]

Empathy

When nurses undertook an 8-weekprogram in mindfulness meditation they found that it facilitated increased empathy for their patients. Additionally they were less prone to take on their patients' negative emotions and therefore experienced less personal negativity as a result of the practice program.[21] Similar benefits were reported by health-care professionals undergoing mindfulness meditation practice. After 8 weeks they found a significant increase in self-compassion along with noticeable stress reduction.[22]

Anxiety

Multiple studies have been conducted on the effects of Mindfulness Meditation in young folk suffering from psychological disturbances. In one these studies, teachers reported an improvement in academic function and the scientists documented a significant decrease in participant anxiety over a 6-week research period.[23]

In another incredible study, fatigue and anxiety were amazingly reduced in participants undergoing a mindfulness meditation program, after just 4 days. Furthermore, this study found an increase in sustained attention and improved executive processing efficiency. This is one of the few studies that have demonstrated lasting positive effects with only 20 minutes of meditation daily in a short space of time. This provides compelling evidence that meditation benefits are readily apparent and accessible in a relatively short time frame, even amongst meditation novices.[24]

Conduct disorder

Adolescents with conduct disorder were able to decrease their aggressive behaviour through using a mindfulness program. The intervention required these youngsters to consciously place their attention on the soles of their feet whenever a stressful situation arose.[25]

Other conditions

Conditions researched that reported decreased symptoms from Mindfulness intervention programs include:[26]

• Chronic Pain - significantly reduced[27]

• IrritableBowel Syndrome– decreased severity of symptoms[28]

• Tinnitus - helped to cope with difficult sensations through acceptance[29]

• Addiction[30] - decreased behaviour, cravings,[31] improved impulse control and counteracted negative self criticism in addicts[32]

- Attention deficit hyperactivity disorder (ADHD)[33]
- Cancer - decreased negative symptoms reported[34]
- Fibromyalgia- modest benefits reported[35]
- HIV- Decreased frequency of symptoms; [36] also buffered CD4+ T lymphocyte declines in HIV-1 infected adults in another study[37]

In general, multiple studies have concluded that mindfulness based interventions decreased symptoms of disease, reduced pain and stress, depression, anxiety and reactivity in many different patients suffering from a wide spectrum of diseases.[38]

Chapter 12: Eleven Buddhist Techniques for Mindfulness

Practicing the art of mindfulness is facilitating your mind to think about things and aspects that you choose. Learning to live in the present moment is focusing on things that are happening in the moment. When you master mindfulness, you learn to observe and see the happenings around the world without judgment.

Emotions are an imperative part of mindfulness and you cannot ignore them at all. However, it is very important that you learn to let go of these emotions.

Technique # 15 – Be aware of what your mind is focusing on – Do not allow yourself to think about things you don't want to.

You have to consciously work so that your mind focuses on things that you want it to focus on.

It is extremely easy to get completely wrapped up in your emotions thinking of various incidents that occurred during the day including those that happened in your personal relationships and also those that happened at work. Practice your mind to focus only on those things that you choose.

You should start by focusing your mind on objects and things in the outside world. And once you get better at this, start focusing on things happening inside you.

Be watchful of your mind wandering away; gently pull it back to that one thing you choose to focus on each time.

Technique # 16 – Watch your actions mindfully – There is a vast difference between knowing what you are doing and being mindful of what you are doing. When you are talking to a friend, you KNOW you are talking to him or her; that is an autopilot mode. But are you MINDFUL of how and what you are talking? Pay close attention to each detail of your actions.

Technique # 17 – Be aware of the purpose of your actions – When you pay attention to details, when you are focused in the present moment; these are ways of being aware of the purpose of your actions.

Pay close attention to what you are thinking; pay close attention to whether what you are thinking is the same as what you are doing; this will help you identify the purpose of your action.

For every action you do, focus on the feelings involved; focus on the minute details of the action, and focus your mind on the present moment.

Technique # 18 – Leave the past behind – How often do you look back in your life and say to yourself, "I wish I had/hadn't done that?" How often do you look back and pine away for something that happened many years ago?

Very often, isn't it? And it you noticed, going back to the past is also on autopilot.

You are peeling potatoes and your mind is thinking about a sad event that happened in your past. Many times, these feelings, whether happy or sad, can bring a smile or tears unknowing to you. It is almost like an impulsive reaction.

Someone else is looking at you and asking you, “Why are you smiling or why are you crying?” Then you wake up and realize you are actually peeling potatoes, but your mind has wandered off. Endeavor to avoid this. While you really cannot control your emotions, at least be aware that your mind is traveling to a place you don’t want it to. Gently bring it back to the peeling of the potato.

Technique # 19 – Do not think of the future – Planning for the future is an important aspect of our lives. “Do not think of the future" does not mean do not plan prudently. It only means that you should not get so caught up with your future that the fears and anxiety with something that may or may not happen tomorrow would affect your state of mind right now.

Planning your future is also an act of the present. Make a to-do list for tomorrow. Focus on making the list to ensure you have noted everything you can think of. Now, put that list away and pick up the to-do list of today. From that pick up the first task and focus your mind and body on doing and completely that task to the best of your abilities.

Technique # 20 – Avoid looking at your watch – It is a very common and unwitting task that we keep repeating ever so often.

We keep looking at our watch to keep track of time. We are checking it even when there is nothing to do. Remember you have no control over time. Whether you do something or you don't do something, time will pass; so don't waste time hassling over time.

Checking the time is fine as long as you do worry yourself about how slowly or how fast the time is passing by. That is your mind working. If you have work to do, do it and be in the present moment. If you do not have work to do, then sit back and relax and even then be in the present moment.

Technique # 21 – Take time off to do nothing at all – Productivity is great, but doing nothing is important too. Take some time off regularly to sit back and do nothing but watch the world go by. By doing nothing, I mean nothing! Don't look at your smartphone; don't watch TV; don't watch a movie; don't read a book; don't eat; don't drink; don't walk; don't run; don't talk; don't do anything; just sit by the window side or any other favorite place of yours and let yourself be!

While you do nothing, you are truly experiencing living and enjoying the world around you. Watch the bird fly by; watch the leaves in the tree rustle; watch the bus going down the road; watch the dog walking contently; watch the waves dashing against the rocks; feel the breeze against your face; feel the ground beneath your feet; feel the warmth of the sun; hear the sound of rustling leaves; hear the sound of a vehicle going by; hear the bark of the dog; hear the laughter of someone nearby; hear the tapping of someone's feet nearby; do nothing but watch, feel, hear, and enjoy everything around you.

Of course, your thoughts will go away somewhere else. Cajole them back to the present moment and observe everything around you. You don't need to record anything - just sit back and do nothing.

Technique # 22 – Do not be judgmental and avoid negativity – When you are in the present moment and living in the moment, enjoy the things around you without passing judgment. Observe the surrounding sights, sounds and smells without passing any kind of judgment. If you smell something that you don't seem like; simply smell and don't pass judgment. If you see something that you like; again just watch and don't pass judgment.

Instead of blaming anyone, see if you can empathize with the person or situation. When you judge something or someone, remember that you are actually predicting the outcome of a present moment and this is not based on anything really true but is based on someone's behavior and your view of it. Just be objective about everything happening around you.

Negativity saps energy, which is already such a limited resource for us. Avoid negative thoughts, ideas, or emotions to the best possible extent.

Technique # 23 – Do not hold on to any emotions; good or bad – Being mindful does not mean being thrilled or excited always. It means letting go of all emotions as much as possible. When you live in the present moment without judgment or without comparing it to something in the past or something that you envision in the future, you will have the power to see and appreciate the positivity around you.

Technique # 24 – Treat your emotions and feelings like how you would treat the weather – Mindfulness means living fully in the present moment without expectations, without fears, without anxieties, etc. However, living a life of mindfulness does not mean stoicism. Embrace your happy emotions, but remember to let them go.

Emotions rise and fade! Let them rise and let them fade. You cannot hold on to them. You cannot control emotions just like you cannot control the weather. If you are thinking that you will control emotions in such a way that you will keep happiness and give away sadness, then you are not living in the present moment. Mindfulness is living in the moment and letting everything else including emotions go.

Technique # 25 – Treat everyone with compassion and kindness – The core of mindful living is compassion and kindness for all around you. As you live your daily life, you are bound to meet people who will think differently from the way you do. You will encounter people who are seemingly better off than you and/or worse off than you. As a practitioner of mindfulness, you must treat everyone with compassion and kindness.

The choice of practicing mindfulness is your personal choice and your personal journey. Letting go of your judgmental attitude is a choice you made and this non-judgmental attitude should be even for those people who choose not to practice mindfulness.

Chapter 13: Basics of Mindfulness Meditation

Getting Started with Meditation

Meditation is immersing yourself in your mind. Imagine it is the sea and your thoughts are the waves. You sink below the waves as though you distance yourself from your thoughts. As you sink further below them, you no longer feel their push and pull on you. Instead, you are in at a very calm place where you can observe them as they ebb and flow. It will take some effort and time to get deeper into your mind but with enough practice, there is no doubt you will get there. Remember that longer periods of formal meditation will help you reach deeper.

Formal practice involves allotting some time in your day to do mindfulness meditation. The amount of time you set is largely your choice, as with the schedule and place. Formal practice is the core of a lifestyle of mindfulness and is a proper place to start for beginners.

Here is a basic routine that you should try:

Mindful Breathing Meditation

This type of meditation as the name implies focuses on how you breathe. It can be used to bring your breathing back to normal whenever you need to.

Here's how you do it:

1. Find a position that you are comfortable with. You can sit on a chair, on the floor; lie down on the bed, whatever position you want. What is important is for you to keep your spine as straight as possible. You can shut your

eyes if this makes you feel comfortable. Remember that this is the time that you have taken out for yourself. It is an opportunity to be in the moment and experience it. You are not here to reach any goals. There is no need to exert too much effort. You only need to experience each moment as they are. Get rid of any physical stress you that you have. Relax yourself.

2. Feel your breathing. Take note of the sensations. Feel yourself inhaling. Notice how the air goes in and out through your nostrils. Turn your attention to how it passes through your throat. Move on to your chest, feel how it rises and falls. Focus on one of these places where you can comfortably feel your breath and keep your focus on it.

3. After a while your mind will probably wander. Ideas and thoughts will eventually flow in along with fantasies and

dreams. This is not a problem. When you notice it happening, your focus must slowly be back to your breathing. Do not get frustrated. Do not judge yourself. Remember that this is all part of the process and it will not be the last time it will happen. When you start feeling cross with yourself, smile about it. Guide yourself back on track as much as necessary.

4. Keep on meditating like this. Try to maintain your breathing. Keep the speed and depth constant.

5. When you are done, you can open your eyes.

You can practice this for as long as you want. It all depends on what you are comfortable with or what your circumstances will allow. It is best to set a definite amount of time to meditate before you start. Commit to this period. To avoid worrying about the time, use a timer or stop watch that has a gentle ring to tell you when the time is up. Focus only on your breathing and avoid interruptions.

Chapter 14: Mindfulness Exercises

Performing mindfulness exercises is a great way to improve your meditation skills. As a beginner, you can start with simple and easy to do exercises. You should also choose the ones that will not take much of your time.

These mindfulness exercises are specifically designed and created to help you develop your ability to stay in the present moment. They are also efficient in helping you improve your ability to focus. The more you practice these exercises, the easier it will be for you to meditate. Over time, your mental muscles will also grow stronger.

One Minute of Mindfulness

This mindfulness exercise can be done in just a minute. Hence, it is perfect if you have a hectic schedule. You can actually do it anytime and anywhere you like. All you have to do is focus all your attention on the way you breathe.

You can look at your watch as you perform this exercise to help you keep track of the time. For the next sixty seconds, you should keep your eyes open and breathe as you normally would. Get ready to catch your mind drifting off and bringing back your attention to your breathing.

This mindfulness exercise may be simple but it is very powerful. In fact, some people take several years before they are able to complete one minute of clear and alert attention.

You should take note that this mindfulness exercise is neither a personal challenge nor some sort of contest. There is no passing or failing at this exercise. You only get to experience it.

You can perform this exercise as many times as you want throughout the day. The more you do it, the better you become at restoring your mind to the present moment and restoring your mind to peace and clarity.

Gradually, you can increase the duration of your exercise. So instead of just one minute, you can perform it for two, three, or four minutes. You can even use a mindfulness bell as an object of your focus instead of your breathing.

A mindfulness bell recording is especially recommended if you tend to struggle with breathing techniques and mantra meditation. It can significantly improve your ability to focus at the present moment and reach a state of mental stillness.

Conscious Observation

This mindfulness exercise involves picking up an object and holding it out in your hands. You can pick up any object you see, such as a cup, a pen, or a ball. Let your attention completely focus on that particular object. However, instead of assessing, studying, or thinking about it, you should simply observe it.

When you do this, you will feel a sense of increased 'nowness' and 'being awake'. You should observe how your mind can quickly release thoughts from your past as well as how different it feels to stay in the moment. This mindfulness exercise is subtle and powerful. You can also practice it with your ears by listening to certain sounds.

The Ten-Second Count

This very simple exercise aims to improve your concentration. However, instead of focusing on your breathing, you have to close your eyes and focus on counting from one to ten. Whenever you catch your mind drifting off, you should go back to number one.

Air on Exposed Skin

This exercise requires you to pay close attention to the feeling of air on your skin for ten to sixty seconds. It makes you practice in the experiential processing mode instead of the judging mode, which tends to be your default mode. To make the exercise easier, you should wear something that exposes a huge portion of your skin, such as a short-sleeved shirt.

Mindfulness Cues

This exercise aims to make you focus on your breathing whenever an environmental cue occurs. You can choose any cue that works well for you. For instance, every time your phone rings, you should bring your attention to the present moment and focus on your breathing. Mindfulness cues are excellent mindfulness techniques that can train you to snap out of your unconscious "autopilot" state of mind and take you back to the present moment.

Chapter 15: Putting it altogether for better you

Meditation looks positively insignificant on the surface. That's because on the surface, it is. The real power of meditation happens on the inside. As mentioned earlier, the practice of meditation relaxes and calms you down, and helps you to better handle stress, or whatever it is that is causing anxiety in your life. Believe it or not, studies have also shown that meditation has the ability to boost test scores and improve brain function, not to mention making you amazingly marvelous. More and more we see people from all walks of life practicing meditation for the many health and mental benefits.

Still, you may be feeling that sitting cross-legged on the floor, or uttering a mantra is silly. Or maybe your cultural or spiritual upbringing keeps you from exploring any meditation practice in the first place. Maybe you feel too busy, and can't make time during your day to practice meditation. Maybe your anxiety is what's holding you back. Whatever it is, no one can force you to meditate. The decision to cross the bridge to a better you, must be yours and yours alone.

We place way too much importance on what, when and how meditation should be. Truthfully, if you can sit, walk or lie down, close your eyes and breathe, you can meditate. The main goal of any meditation is to relax. Unfortunately, there are a lot of stressed-out people who have a difficult time just learning to relax. That's the beauty of meditation.

The fact that we are a society of "worker-bees," checking our watch or cell phone every three-seconds has become second nature. This makes it very difficult to sit still, even for minutes at a time. Meditation is all about allowing yourself to a few free minutes, alone and all to yourself without distractions. The more you practice meditation and give yourself those few precious minutes you deserve, the easier it will be to sit still for longer periods of time. In fact, once you get the knack, you will crave these times of solitude.

While "trying" to meditate (we'll assume you're giving meditation a shot or at least collecting information) you may find you just can't turn-off your mind. Frankly, it doesn't matter if you can't completely clear you mind of all thoughts, or your mind continues to race about every little thing that happened during your day. Meditation practices are called "practices" for a reason. If you find yourself wandering to things like, what's for dinner, or the fact you juts failed your Biology test, try to return to your breathing and relax; let yourself be.

Some people find meditation boring. Or at least they find it boring when they try meditation for the first time. This is understandable when we are so conditioned as a society to being entertained by a television or YouTube video. But once you let yourself relax and realize how enjoyable it can be to be silent and still, you may find yourself turning off and tuning out of the distractions around you.

If you have not yet tried meditation or if you have tried it but find yourself unwilling to try it again, it may be an internal fear of letting go and exposing your feelings and emotions. It is human nature to walk away from anything that makes us feel uneasy. Interestingly, it is this fear that is one of the basic reasons to try meditation. It helps us to face the things that make us anxious or jittery: a new job, a new relationship, flying on an airplane for the first time, or settling into a new home. Meditation takes the edge off, and allows us to let go of those things we fear the most.

While there may be things that hold you back from trying something new, the need in all of our lives for mindful meditation is real. There are no cut-and-dried formulas that will work for everyone. People are as unique and different as each practice of meditation. Flexibility is key. No part of your physical or mental life should be left out of our practice of meditation. Every aspect is important and should be practiced, like the first time riding a bike. If you fall off the first time, you have to get back up and try again, because if you don't at least try to make a conscience effort, you may forever wonder what you are missing. Just as you may want to learn how to live with anxiety, or how to find relief from your tension headaches without prescribed medication, if you want to learn how to swim you have to get into the water.

A recent hands-on experience put much of this into perspective for a co-worker. Let's call him Dan. For some time, Dan had been experiencing monthly, and oftentimes weekly, panic attacks. Although he hid them well from his co-workers, it was obvious that something was interfering with his work. He would often go missing from his desk, and when he returned, he'd be sweaty and flush. His co-workers actually thought he may be experimenting with drugs. One afternoon while sitting at his desk, Dan grabbed his chest and said he thought he may be having a heart attack. They called 911, and he was rushed to the hospital. As it turned out, thankfully Dan did not have a heart attack, but instead the doctors agreed he had had a panic attack. They told him he should see a psychiatrist if the attacks continued or became worse, and they would put him on prescribed medication.

When Dan returned to work, he finally admitted that for year he had been suffering from chronic panic attacks and anxiety, thus the reason for his absence at work. One of the women in the office asked Dan if he had ever heard of, or tried meditation. As Dan is a natural skeptic, he laughed and said meditation was foolish, and only meant for simple-minded hippies. With much restraint, his co-worker, Barb, calmly disagreed and admitted she had been practicing mindful meditation for years. Although still a bit suspicious, she eventually got his attention and Dan decided to give it a try.

For the first week, Dan tried "walking meditation". He would take a break at the same time every morning and walk for about 15-minutes. He said he tried to concentrate, as much as possible, on simply walking and the simple cadence of putting one foot in front of the other. When Dan returned to the office, however, he said walking was too distracting. He found it difficult to concentrate on just walking and swinging his arms because of all the other people on the sidewalk, or cars rushing by. Barb told him to try walking on a trail or in a secluded place; away from people and distractions, but Dan had given up and decided all forms of meditation were silly and just not worth his time.

That's when Dan experienced another heart-pounding panic attack and made an appointment with a psychiatrist. The doctor prescribed medication, and for a while Dan seemed better, until we noticed his worsening depression, and he complained about dizziness and confusion. Barb stepped back in.

This time Barb advised Dan to try "sitting meditation". So, Dan asked our boss if he could borrow his office when he left the building at noon for a lunch break. Barb told Dan to take a wooden chair from the break room, to sit straight in the chair with his feet on the floor, close his eyes and try to only concentrate on his breathing — nothing else. But as soon as the office phone rang, Dan ran out of the office and said trying to concentrate on his breathing with phones ringing and people talking was making him angry, and only added to his frustration.

Barb then suggested he sit in his car, which he did, for nearly a week. He said it was difficult sitting in the front seat as he was distracted by all the buttons and gadgets on the dashboard, so he tried sitting in the backseat. He found it was easier to concentrate from the backseat, but Dan was still upset he was so easily bothered by every little thing outside. To him, he had failed at something he thought ridiculous in the first place. Again, Barb stepped in.

This time, with Barb's encouragement, Dan tried sitting meditation at home. At the same time every evening, in a comfortable chair, with his feet on the ground, Dan meditated. He focused his attention on the flame of a candle, and breathed. After just two weeks, Dan sensed a change, and so did his co-workers.

Months later, Dan continues to practice sitting meditation. Although he still experiences bouts of anxiety, his panic attacks have all but stopped. When he begins to feel anxious at work or at home, he now simply closes his eyes and breaths. It no longer matters where he is, and he is no longer distracted by things around him.

Dan is more relaxed. He now excitedly defends and promotes meditation techniques, and has researched and tried many different practices. Dan is a believer, and only one of the many thousands that have found relief from chronic anxiety.

Chapter 16: Using Mindfulness Daily for Maximum Benefits

Mindfulness meditation can be practiced anywhere at any time. Because of that it can and should be used daily. By having mindful awareness throughout your day, you can have an awareness of your thought patterns and you can break the patterns that have been affecting your daily decision-making. As you use the technique on a regular basis, you will find your ability to focus becomes sharper, depression becomes more manageable, stress and anxiety levels go down, and everything begins to change in positive ways.

Mindfulness is a lifestyle. Mindfulness can improve relationships, productivity in the work place, efficiency, and creativity. This is because mindfulness teaches us to focus on facts in the current moment, not worrying about the past or the future. Mindfulness improves the power of your brain.

You could start your day with a mindful meditation or some form of stretching exercise, such as yoga or Pilates, have mini meditations throughout the day, and end your day with a formal meditation exercise or a simple breathing exercise to help you get to sleep. It doesn't matter how you structure your routine as long as you remember to practice mindfulness somewhere in your day, every day. The more you practice the better your life will become. If you find you forget, leave reminders for yourself, set an alarm, ask a friend to remind you, or use any method that helps jog your memory.

Remind yourself why it is so important to get into a habit of having daily mindful meditations. Remember that meditation can lower blood pressure, lower stress levels, improve your immune system, improve your relationships, help you have better emotional control, improve brain function, and promote peace and relaxation. Because mindful meditation helps you to slow down and think about your reactions before they occur, you may be able to solve your problems more creatively and with less negative long-term effects.

The hardest part of mindful meditation is letting go of thoughts, feelings, and emotions once you have acknowledged them. By doing meditation, that focuses on a specific task or even breathing, you break the cycle of your thoughts and tell your mind that it's time to stop the vicious negative thought-cycle. It's hard at first but it does get easier with practice; another reason why it so important to practice mindfulness as a regular routine.

Chapter 17: Journaling For Total Awareness

Detail, Detail, Detail!

Journaling, for your purposes, is the best and most consistent way to stay mindful.Here if the note we'll end on for mindfulness living.

Keep a journal with excruciating detail. The ultimate physical manifestation of your mindfulness will be in this notebook. Use it during self-reflection, for the streamline of consciousness, and for random thoughts that may offer insight to your state of being. This will help you tap into what makes you sad, what lifts your spirits, and will give you great insight to what you're feeling, and what kinds of things trigger you to have certain thoughts.

Where Do I Start?

Here are some questions to ask yourself while journaling:

1.) How do you feel when you exercise?

2.) What happened on the days or during the days before you were feeling depressed, happy, anxious, stressed?

3.) What are your short term goals?

4.) What are your goals for the long term?

5.) What can you do to reach these goals with the time you have during your day? How can you make more time without adding unreasonable stress to your life?

Your journal, if you allow it, can be the key to your mind. This is because it will include obvious thoughts, background thoughts, and details that may not be immediately noticeable. If you jot them down, you have the option of reflecting on them later.

Make sure you keep it in a safe place, or include a lock with it, to ease your fears that someone may read it. This journal is for you, and will be safe from anyone else's eyes.

Keeping a journal will allow you to pick up on things going through your mind that you may only be able to see after time away from your thoughts, self-reflection, or that only become apparent after the fact. Not only will you be able to claim mindfulness and ease the stressors in your day, but you will also learn a great deal about yourself in the process. It might also be good to leave yourself notes and messages of reinforcement. If you do it with purpose, and you keep your goal of mindfulness in sight, journaling could change your life.

Chapter 18: How to Overcome Them Obstacles

Positively living in your “now” isn't simple, yet it is very rewarding. The most ideal approach to get up and go on your own way, "without a moment's hesitation," is to comprehend the potential deterrents and plan ahead of time on how you'll manage them.

Mindfulness Requires Progressing Exertion

Mindfulness takes a great deal of work. However, the fortunate thing is that the more time you drill, the less demanding it gets, and the more cheerful your life gets to be. From the start, your musings will be in insane, and everything will appear to be crazy. Your circumstance will feel vulnerable. But the more you concentrate on being where you are completely, the simpler it will be to discover true serenity in the given moment and time. Mindfulness is best accomplished when it is practiced throughout the day. It's not only for when you take a seat and contemplate. Concentrate on being aware of your contemplations when you're doing ordinary assignments and it will be simpler to stay mindful when things get extreme.

There Will Be Diversions

When you're on your excursion to getting more aware of your own self, it appears to be as though the universe begins tossing stuff at you simply to provide you challenges. The preoccupations could be issues throughout your life, show in your connections, or old negative convictions popping up from your past. These are incredible open doors to practice living in the moment. They will help you in becoming stronger, better, and all the more in tune with yourself. The issues and difficulties we face are, in actuality, educators. They are there to help you to develop and to acknowledge who you actually are.

Advancement Doesn't Generally Come Rapidly

Advancement may appear to be excruciatingly abated. There will be times when you join to things and circumstance that you need, which will make it difficult to be completely in the moment. It's difficult to be careful when you're failing to move on or fixating on what's to come. We all do those things some of the time. I've encountered it endless times in my own life. The more I need something, the more I focus on not having it and needing to get it. When I discharge the connection and concentrate on being thankful for what I already have, my life appears to shift, and advancement appears to happen regularly.

You May Need To Surrender

Like with any beneficial adventure, you will have a craving for surrendering and giving up numerous times. It is through these times that you feel most baffled that you are nearly a leap forward. Our lives are very similar to the seasons. We experience chilly, dull winters and upbeat, stretching summers. Everything goes back and forth. It's the rhythmic movement of life. When you understand that the testing times are there to help you develop, you will naturally feel more quiet and loose.

Your Objectives May Challenge Your Mindfulness

Having objectives is phenomenal, key even, yet when you get to be excessively connected to them, something terrible happens. You realize that you're over-attached when you begin feeling confused, furious, and negative. Connection tangles our clarity. You are seeking after your objectives on the grounds that you accept that they will make you euphoric. Keep that in mind when you begin letting your objectives pull you into an upsetting state of psyche. On the off chance that you concentrate on the great things around you, you'll feel that satisfaction that you think you have to pursue. This will make you much more content in the long haul, and, obviously, at this time.

You May Overlook That The Journey Is The Goal

Most individuals miss the fact that the fun of a journey is not in the destination, but in the journey itself. Have you ever perceived that when you achieve an objective, it is not as energizing as you thought it would be? Of course, it feels incredible to hit a turning point, but in the event that you don't supplant that objective with another, you will soon end up feeling unfulfilled. People need objectives so they can have a feeling of reason and satisfaction. It is in during the adventure that we learn, develop, and get better.

When you're honing mindfulness, recollect that there is no place to touch base. In the event that you concentrate on what is going on at this time, the rest will deal with itself. Indeed, the most qualified experts on Earth need to manage troublesome circumstances and disorganized musings. The distinction is that they have figured out how to acknowledge the minute for what it is. When you do this, you turn into the gatekeeper of your internal space, which is the best way to feel great inside and discover significant serenity at this moment.

Chapter 19: Keeping Inner Peace

Let your soul expand, let your heart reach

out to others in loving and generous warmth,

and great and lasting will be your joy, and

all prosperity will come to you.

– James Allen

It's hard to explain how important it is for every each of us to find and maintain inner peace. We already described what inner peace, but we haven't explained how to reach it while taming your anxiety.

Day 7: Inner Peace

Reminders before you take the journey:

- Reaching inner peace isn't easy. It's a difficult journey, one that will test your perseverance and desire.
- It is a process; therefore, don't expect to reach inner peace after just 7 days. You need to do this every day.
- You can only find inner peace if you are ready to accept it.

Here are the steps ti finding and keeping inner peace.

- Know your state of mind

As mentioned before, be aware of what you are thinking. Learn how to remove all negative thoughts and welcome positive ones.

- Acceptance

Know that there are things that you can't change no matter what. Accept this fact and try to work with it. Find peace rather than destroying your peace of mind by over thinking.

- Work with anxiety

Rather than refusing anxiety and your environment, try to work with it. You don't have to go against the flow, but you can strive to join it and flourish using your unique side.

- Take it simple

Living in simplicity can do wonders for your peace of mind. A cluttered life is a sign of a cluttered anxiety-induced life. Let go of unnecessary things.

- Give and forgive and forget

This is a very simple strategy but quite hard for many. Learn how to give and find inner fulfillment. Forgive people and see how peaceful you become. Forget the pain and welcome the love. You'll be surprised how much more you will receive while finding and maintaining inner peace.

Chapter 20: mindful yoga

Balancing the body-mind

From this chapter, we will take mindfulness into the real world. We will learn to work mindfully, eat mindfully... and be mindful with each and every activity. The best way to start it is by practicing few simple yoga postures. Yoga has become widely popular for its numerous health benefits. Anyone can practice yoga; you won't require any equipment. A yoga mat will be helpful but not mandatory. Why combining mindfulness with yoga? Because yoga focuses on balancing, and balancing is essential if you want to bring mindfulness in your working life. Besides, yoga postures are more than physical exercises. If you want to move your body mindfully, start practicing mindful yoga and in time all your movements will be mindful. The following yoga postures will improve the flexibility of your body as well as longevity. Also, if you are dealing with stress and depression, you will find the following poses very helpful. But our primary goal from those exercises is learning to move in a mindful way. So far we have practiced mindfulness in a still posture, this time, we will practice it while moving.

Moving mindfully with Yoga

Wear loose, soft and comfortable clothing during this exercise. Yoga has to be practiced in bare feet, in empty stomach or at least a couple of hours after a heavy meal. You can practice yoga anytime of the day but the ideal time is morning.

Mountain poses (Tadasana)

Stand straight with heels slightly apart and make sure that your weight is evenly distributed on your feet. Keep your gaze straight, so that your chin is parallel to the floor. Place your head aligning to the center of your pelvis. Now breathe in and raise your hands from the sides with palms facing each other, lift your chin at the same time and fix your gaze on the ceiling. Now join the palms together and breathe out. Now breathe naturally and stay in this posture for thirty seconds. Pay your complete attention while moving your body, and feel the pressure in your joints and muscles while you are resting in the posture and stay with the feeling.

Child Pose (Balasana)

Sit on your heels with your sheen and knee touching the ground. Breathe in and bend your body at the waist, straighten your hands and rest your palms on the floor slightly apart. Now your forehead is touching the ground. Pay your attention to your forehead and breath naturally. Stay in this position for thirty seconds. Feel the stress in your back, shoulders, and your hands. Allow your head to rest comfortably on the floor, and inhale and exhale in a natural way. Be fully present with this experience and once you are done, switch to the next pose. Child pose relieves anxiety and anger and prevents back pain.

Thunderbolt poses (Vajrasana)

From child pose move to the sitting posture while breathing in. Make sure that you heels are positioned either side of your anus. If you find it difficult to stay like this, you can place a pillow either underneath your sheet or between the heels and buttocks. Keep your back straight, chin up and parallel to the floor and rest your palms on your knees. Some practitioners prefer to close their eyes during the postures to pay total focus. Inhale and exhale naturally, but be present with the experience. Thirty seconds should be enough, but if you are comfortable with this posture, you can stay few minutes. You can sit in Thunderbolt pose immediately after a heavy meal to accelerate digestion and to get rid of extra fat around your waistline. Thunderbolt pose improves confidence if you can do it mindfully. Once you are done, practice the following postures.

Cat-cow pose

From thunderbolt, pose lifts your thighs and bring them perpendicular to the floor.

Touch the floor with your palms. Now your hands are parallel to your thighs, and your torso is parallel to the floor, in a table-top position. Hands apart, knees apart.... Take a deep breath. Breathe out and stretch your torso round up towards the sky, lower your head at the same time. Spend more time in exhaling and keep the pressure on your belly...let your belly contract with exhalation. Now this position is similar to a cat stretching out. This is cat pose (Marjaryasana).

Spend five seconds in cat pose, while you are breathing out.

Now keep breathing in slowly while you stretch your belly toward the floor with curving your body from the waist, raising your chest and lifting the chin at the same time. Gaze up, chest up and spine curved towards the floor. This is cow pose (Bitilasana).

If your attention drifts away, calmly drift back and focus on the movements. Breath out, round your torso and slowly move to cat pose... breath-in... lower your belly... gently move to the cow pose. Practice these postures back to back. While exhaling change your position to cat pose... while inhaling... switch to cow pose. Do not inhale or exhale in-between. Inhaling (cow-pose) for five seconds... Exhaling (cat-pose) for five seconds. Rest your focus on the movements, and the stress points.

The above exercises are very easy to do yoga Asanas and an excellent way to bring mindfulness from meditation to the real life. If you do better in mindful yoga, you will do great in other activities because you've learned how to move mindfully.

Chapter 21: Goodbye to Depression and Anxiety

The specters of depression and anxiety have the full propensity to become almost like a living force that haunts our lives. We face multiple stressors each and every day of our existence. We all face stress and hardship, the key to success lies in how we deal with that stress and hardship. There is also such a thing as good stress and bad stress.

That's right, not all stress is bad, and we need a little bit of it just to stay motivated. Just think about it! Don't you work harder when you have a deadline and some kind of outside force that expects something of you? This kind of stress is good because it can push you to come up with some of your best work.

But this good stress can very easily swing in the other direction and become bad stress if we're not careful. And bad stress has the opposite effect of motivation. It can debilitate and paralyze us. Along with the already mentioned efforts in mindful mediation and positive feedback loops, we need to be able to "re-perceive" the things that make us anxious and depressed.

When we are able to re-evaluate the things that made us so anxious in the past, we can gain access to more data than what we were previously comfortable with examining. In this state of re-perception, the trend towards experiential avoidance becomes much less automatic, and instead of avoiding, you find yourself confronting stressors head on and re-examining from a non-biased perspective exactly what it was that made you so stressed out in the first place.

The process of re-perceiving stimuli stops maladaptive habits right in their tracks. Once we learn to stop being ruled by our emotions, we can think before we act, allowing us to not be automatically sucked up into habitual reactive patterns. In this way when anxiety does occur, we can passively recognize it for what it is without being consumed by it. Instead of being ruled by our emotional triggers, we can be the master of them.

The key to eliminating depression and anxiety is realizing that they are not some static state of being. Anxiety and depression are merely part of a procedure, part of a process, and these processes begin with some sort of trigger. Everything is fine and then a truck aggressively tailgates you. This is a trigger point for the process of anxiety. You have to get to the root of this chain of worry before the process spirals out of control. Mindful awareness short circuits this process.

Without being controlled by our fears and anxieties, we can be mindfully aware of them and further use them as useful pieces of information that foster better understanding and sense of well being. When you enlighten yourself to the realty of the impermanence of all mental states, when you realize that all things will pass, then you will be able to much handle and tolerate unpleasant states in a much easier fashion.

Re-perceiving allows us to view our own mental commentary in the face of stressors from a neutral footing. It's as if we are acting as a reader our own liner notes in life without being directly affected by it. It frees us to see the present moment for what it really is without overly reacting from prior habit, conditioning, prejudice, or experience. Through this direct exposure the experiencer is able to face their deepest fears and regain their inner peace. Through a sheer effort of mindfulness, you truly can say goodbye to anxiety and depression for good.

Chapter 22: Being More Aware and Accepting of Life Challenges

We have no control over some of the things that happen in our lives, it doesn't even matter how much you try to do so. Some people would complain about their situation; saying things like, "why is life so unfair?", or "I don't deserve this kind of thing," and things of that nature. However, what good will come out from complaining about things that are beyond your control? The answer is nothing; you will get absolutely nothing when you complain. Instead of whining how things aren't going your way, you should just accept things as they are.

How to be more accepting of Life's Challenges

"The more you resist, the more you'll suffer." Just accept the fact that life isn't perfect. There will always be times when things just won't go your way no matter how hard you try. It's like crossing a raging river; instead of wasting your strength trying to swim in a straight line towards the opposite shore, it is actually better to let the water carry you and just try to steer yourself towards the other river bank a little further downstream.

"Not getting what you want is just a part of the larger plan in life." Who knows? Maybe the reason why you weren't able to get the last pair of the pants you have had your eyes on since last month meant that another person would be wearing it to a job interview. Don't think that life denied you an opportunity, believe that someone needed it more than you did.

"These are just curve balls that life throws every once in a while." What do you think will happen if everything in your life went the way you wanted them to? If you take away the unexpected things, life would be incredibly boring. Sure, everything you set out to do will always be a success, but where's the challenge in that?

Remember, nothing good ever comes out of resisting your fate. Sure, there will be times when you should fight your circumstances, but that's only when you know you can make a difference. For instance, if your boss is giving you a hard time at work, you can communicate with your boss, or if he/she isn't amicable to having a discussion, you can escalate your case to Human Resources. In this instance, you can do something to improve your situation.

On the other hand, if you're having a bad day because heavy rains meant that you have to cancel that beach trip you have been looking forward to all summer, just accept your circumstance and make the best out of it. Instead of moping around inside you home, put on your swimsuit and frolic around in the rain. It may not be the same as relaxing on the beach, but it can still be just as fun.

Practice mindfulness; stop thinking about what could have happened should things go your way and start living in the moment. Stop trying to control everything because it's impossible. Embrace and accept life's challenges, have faith that everything will be fine in the end.

Chapter 23: Meditation And Clearing The Mind

Meditation and Mindfulness always go hand in hand. Meditation is the act or practice where in an individual trains his mind, or enters into an induced mode of consciousness, to attain absolute awareness. It is the cessation of the thought process. Some consider meditation as a way of life, a state of consciousness wherein the mind is free from irrelevant thoughts and patterns.

To start meditating, one must have a clear mind. To reach a clear state of mind without any interruptions or disruptions seems like a difficult thing to achieve. But there are steps that one can follow to be able to achieve a peaceful, calm, and clear state of mind, ready to undergo the act of meditation.

Relaxing your Body

A relaxed body is essential in undertaking a session of meditation. A relaxed body helps the mind also attain a relaxed state. There are proven ways to relax that are simple enough to follow:

1. Take a minute and go outside to have a walk. Breathe in some fresh air, feel the nature as you stroll. Let the nature calm your nerves and release the heavy tension in your body.

2. Indulge yourself in taking a short nap in the afternoon. Napping is a great way to energize and relax. It eases the tense, aching muscles in your body and reduces stress.

3. Drink a glass of warm milk or green herbal tea. Milk contains a special type of acid that can help you sleep better and relax, while green tea has ingredients that are proven to help prevent cholesterol,

lower blood pressure, and soothes and relaxes your body.

Quiet Location

Try to find a good location where you can practice your meditation. It needs to be quiet and exude an aura of peace. It could be anywhere, from a park, your own room, or any place you are sure of you will be able to concentrate without any distractions, like loud pets, small children, or even the appliances that could emit noise.

For your regular sessions of meditation, delegate a place and make it your official meditation haven. It needs to be a place that connects perfectly with you, also giving you a sense of security and comfort.

Breathing Techniques

Identify a spot in your place to do this. You can roll out a mat, towel, or rug on the floor and take your seat, you can sit in the common Indian-style position or any other position that you feel more comfortable with. Start breathing in and out, slowly. In time you will start feeling relaxed and calm.

To help you on your breathing, you can try to count while you inhale and exhale the air around you. For every breath you take, count it as one. For every exhale, count it as two then repeat. If a thought happens to pass through your mind while doing this, just let it pass.

While also doing this, focus on one thing only. This will allow the brain to easily clear the entire mind, since you are only thinking of one thing, rather than having a head full of thoughts.

Doing this, you will realize that you are getting closer to achieving the state of complete calmness and tranquility. Try to practice this exercise daily. You will find out that in time, if you are practicing this often, you are blocking out the external world a whole lot easier.

Chapter 24: Bring Peace to Everyday Life

The process of introducing mindfulness into your daily life can alleviate stress and anxiety brought on by the hectic demands of a busy world. Many people have to work more than one job just to make ends meet. Add family activities, childcare or caring for an aging parent in the mix and it can mean more stress than seems humanly possible to tolerate.

Mindfulness meditation can bring a level of comfort and contentment that you have never before experienced. It works by centering and focusing calm tranquility from the core of the body and mind. You are better able to handle the attacks of everyday stress to the outer edge of your being.

Releasing your mind of feeling judgment for things happening to and around you has a magical way of bringing freedom. Complete release from worry and using the time to closely observe circumstances brings about wisdom to life that is priceless. You will no longer be ruled by fear or harried by stress and anxiety.

Taking a moment to stand back and observe things happening around you without actively participating can give you a whole new perspective. Have you ever noticed how much of the scenery you miss when you drive a vehicle? Take the time to ride life in the passenger seat occasionally and simply enjoy the view.

Living in the moment each and every day means that distractions will no longer blind you to the brilliance of a colorful sunset or the smell of a fresh ocean breeze. Each experience will be realized to the fullest extent possible. It enriches life by heightening the senses and sensory perception capabilities. It frees the mind to fully absorb the experience of every moment without guilt or lack of awareness.

How many times have you walked or driven somewhere to not even remember the trip? Taking the body and mind off of auto-pilot is the only way to live life to the fullest extent possible. You will be less likely to miss out on the important little details that make life more interesting.

Imagine being able to boost memory, increase creativity, stabilize moods and have an overall feeling of constant well-being. It can elevate levels of self-control for behavior, establish deeper empathy for humanity and create a desire to be more involved on every level. Live a more enriched life with the simple techniques of mindfulness meditation.

Chapter 25: Strength Focus

By focusing on your strengths, you give yourself the chance to feel better and stop being so negative about life! For this, you should ask yourself the following:

1. What is one thing that you do that you know you do better than anyone else?

2. What are the advantages in life that you know you have?

3. What connections do you have?

4. How do you think you're able to influence people?

5. What do most people see as your strengths?

6. Which personal resources do you have access to?

By answering these questions, you get to analyze yourself more—and understand what you need to do to reach your goals!

Chapter 26: Mindfulness Breathing Exercise

When performing mindful meditation it is critical to keep your focus on the present while refraining from having any biased or negative emotions. In order to focus your attention on the present and accepting it without judgment, the anchor of the exercise should always be firm concentration on your breathing. Since breathing is a bodily function that we can fully control or regulate, it is one of the most vital tools for achieving a very clear and relaxed state of mind.

If done properly, mindful breathing can help you feel invigorated, experience heightened awareness, provide a needed energy boost, and reduce anxiety as a natural tranquilizer. Whether you are a novice or expert at meditation, the following is a simple breathing exercise that can be completed within 15 to 20 minutes to ensure you reach the highest level of mindfulness.

1. Begin by finding a quiet and comfortable place to sit on the floor with your body fully supported by a mat or pillow. Be sure to sit in a stable position so that your bones are effortlessly supporting your muscles without strain. It is recommended that you keep your back straight, your shoulder blades gently dropped, and your chin slightly tucked towards your chest. Once you are comfortable, take three slow and easy deep breaths to relax and consciously release all tensions that you are carrying with you.

2. Then, gently let your eyelids close or partially close, whichever is preferable to you for achieving your state of mindfulness. Place your hand over your heart for a moment as a reminder that you will be bringing kindness and gratitude to your breathing. Form an image of your body sitting down and note your posture as if you are viewing yourself from the outside. Gently bring your attention internally to feel the pulsation, vibration, and sensation as they are.

3. Now, focus your concentration on your breathing. Position the tip of your tongue against the ridge of tissue behind your upper front teeth and exhale through your mouth around your tongue while pursing your lips. Close your mouth and inhale quietly through your nose, hold your

breath for a count of seven, and then exhale completely through your mouth making a whoosh sound around your tongue once more.

4. While continuing to breathe in this cycle to inhale and exhale more deeply, pay attention to where you are feeling your breathing most easily. Although some individuals feel it at the nostrils or on the upper lips, others sense it in the chest rising or the abdomen expanding and contracting with each breath. Gently explore your body to discover where your breathing is easiest to notice and when you feel your breath more strongly.

5. As you focus on the feeling of each inhalation and exhalation, feel the air coming into your nostrils and out through your mouth in a whoosh. Let your body

begin to breathe in this cycle automatically and play attention to the sensations of the air each time, one breath after another. Then, reflect on the breathing sensations with kindness while you become aware of how the breath is nourishing your body.

6. Although it is certain that your mind will wander away from the breathing sensations multiple times throughout the exercise and perhaps every minute, it is important to never worry about how often your mind wanders. Simply accept the thoughts that come to mind, accept them without judgment, and gently return to the feeling of your breathing. Move your focus back to experiencing the air coming in your nostrils and out your mouth in a slow, deep breath.

7. After 15 to 20 minutes of mindful breathing, gently begin to open your eyes while continuing to breathe in the slow manner. Be sure to savor the stillness and tranquility of the moment while spreading gratitude throughout your entire body. Now, you are ready to move on to the rest of your day with an increase in vital energy, alertness, concentration, and clarity.

Lightning Source UK Ltd.
Milton Keynes UK
UKHW050008091020
371228UK00005BA/414

9 781989 682272